RICH BY CHOICE

RICH BY CHOICE
Seven Steps to Financial Success

Erlend Peterson, CFP

SEVEN LOCKS PRESS

Santa Ana, California
Minneapolis, Minnesota
Washington, D.C.

Seven Locks Press
P.O. Box 25689
Santa Ana, CA 92799
(800) 354-5348

Printed in the United States of America

Library of Congress Cataloging-in-Publication Data
Peterson, Erlend, 1930–
    Rich by choice: seven steps to financial success / Erlend Peterson.
        p. cm.
    ISBN 0-929765-99-0
        1. Finance, Personal 2. Wealth I. Title
    HG179.P4427 2001
    322.024'01--dc21   2001041082

Cover and Interior Design: Sparrow Advertising & Design
Editorial Services: PeopleSpeak

This book is dedicated to the millions of
middle-class Americans who can be rich if they choose to be.

Contents

List of Tables

Acknowledgments

I did not create this alone. I don't type. But my wife, Joan, types like a tiger; she has typed and retyped this book many times and added her comments and corrections. To Joan go my greatest thanks and admiration. She never stopped smiling.

For expert technical advice, I thank three longtime friends and fellow financial advisors: Steve Libuser, J.D.; John Edmonds, CFP; and especially my business associate and partner, Michael Laine, CFP, Registered Principal and Investment Advisor Affiliate.

Erlend Peterson, CFP

March 2001

Introduction

If I asked you if you were rich, would you say no? But have you ever thought about being rich, about having all the money you wanted?

Of course you have. At some time, everybody has thought about being rich. Some people think about it most of the time.

Our whole society seems to be driven by money. Politicians often talk about economic policy, which is a way of referring to money and individual wealth. Most of the news out of Washington has to do with money: government spending (which gives money to individuals) and taxes (which take money away from individuals) and economic policy. Supposedly, the ideal economic policy would provide plenty of money for everybody.

But what about you? What would you have to do to have all the money you wanted? There are five ways to acquire lots of money: marry it, inherit it, steal it, win it in a lottery, or work for it. The only one of these methods that you can absolutely control is the last one—working for it. But isn't that what everyone is doing? And everyone is not rich. So maybe everyone, or almost everyone, is doing something wrong.

Let's take a look at wealth and see what it is. This book is concerned with financial wealth—money in the bank, or liquid investments. Some people would use a broader definition of wealth that includes good health and good friends, and I would agree with that. A true definition of wealth would include abundance in all areas of life, including friendships and love, family, resources, and money. All of these are a part of wealth, and we must be aware of them. As you accumulate financial wealth, don't forget that true happiness and satisfaction don't come solely from having money but include friendship and health and love. We are, however, concerned here primarily with building financial wealth and becoming rich, rich by choice.

My purpose in this book is to show you how and help you to achieve real financial wealth—$2,000,000. Anyone can do this during his or her working years while buying a house, raising a family, and planning for retirement, which all take a lot of money. *Rich by Choice* shows you how to accomplish all of those goals and still wind up rich and ready to retire.

To become rich takes real personal star quality and perseverance. It is much easier to be poor and mediocre, one of the crowd. If your friends aren't getting rich, why should you? If you were rich, people might expect more of you, and maybe you are not willing to give more.

Yet the truth is that anybody can become rich. It's really very simple. Probably nobody ever told you that before, so you never considered it, but you can become rich if you have some time. Two million dollars may seem like a tremendous amount of money, and it is if you think in terms of getting it all at once. But if you think you can become rich and you set out to do it, you can make it happen. Becoming wealthy is no different from all the other goals people set out to achieve—to get a college education, for example, or to buy a home or to start their own business.

The beauty of learning how to become rich is that everything you do, every choice you make from now on, can help you on your quest. You can still live the life you did before, but now—with your choice of building wealth firmly in mind and your goal of becoming rich, of having $2,000,000 in liquid assets—everything you do will speed you toward your goal.

First is the matter of ownership. Choosing to be rich means that you don't rent or lease, you buy. You choose to own. You must own cash, checking accounts, mutual funds, stocks, and your home and vehicles. Well chosen and well cared for, all of these possessions will *increase* in value because of inflation. Nobody ever grew rich putting money in banks; however, the people who *own* banks can become very rich. Ownership is the first key to wealth.

Next, you have to learn to use inflation and tax laws properly. This also involves a lot of choices. Wise choices will also move you along the path to riches.

You must also learn the simple basics of investing with compound interest. The magic of compound interest is all you need to make your money grow. Using compound interest properly is like walking on a moving sidewalk in an airport. You get where you're going that much faster!

Becoming wealthy takes time. Time is the final element you need to be successful, to become rich. The sooner you start toward your goal, the sooner you will get there. You cannot become rich in five years starting with nothing. Anyone who has ever done it had special skills or expertise or was just plain lucky. But you *can* become rich if you learn the basic principles and follow the seven steps demonstrated in this book and give yourself some time.

This book is the result of 28 years of working face-to-face with people and their financial problems. These are middle-class working people like you and me. They are of all colors and backgrounds, and they all needed to build financial security.

The seven-step financial planning process described here evolved from my years of experience with these wonderful people. Though each person's life and story are different, these seven steps worked for all of them, and they will work for you, too.

The greatest joy of my professional life is seeing the look of delight, of sheer joy, on clients' faces when I tell them that they have reached their goal—for example, they now can retire at full pay—or they have reached an important milestone, such as having a million dollars. For most people, that is a major achievement, a dream come true.

Rich by Choice will show you how and help you to achieve your financial goals while leading a normal life.

This book is not a fast read. You may have read some financial books that are good stories and quick to read, but now you are reading this one because the other books didn't make you rich. Well, this book can. We're going to go slowly, but you're going to be rich because of it.

So read on.

Part 1
Getting Started

Four personal financial situations are presented from the broad spectrum of middle-income people. These people all succeeded in becoming rich. We show how they started and how you can get started, using the seven basic steps of the financial planning process.

Chapter 1
Rich or Poor, It's Your Choice

All the mysteries of accumulating wealth are revealed in this book. By reading this book, you can decide to be rich. You can become rich by choice. To do it, you will have to make a series of choices—some easy, some very difficult. The rich people around you have made the right choices. Let their example encourage you to always do likewise. Also remember that *most* of the people around you will continue to make the wrong choices.

The first choice you have is whether to adopt a mind-set or attitude of wealth, of richness. Do you want to be rich? Are you willing to become rich, to have all the money you need and to take responsibility for that and all it entails? If you say, "Yes, I do," then you *will* become rich. Everything you do from now on must include the fact that you are heading toward being rich. Don't say, "I want my kids to be rich someday." Instead say, "I am going to be rich when I retire," and then you can retire at 65 or 55 or even 45. The choices are up to you.

Let me define "rich" the way we are going to use it in this book. Having a big house does not mean you are rich. Driving a big, expensive car does not mean you are rich. You might be just showing off. Taking long vacations doesn't mean you are rich, either. These luxuries are yours to enjoy if you are rich. However, if you are not yet rich, they may stand in the way of your becoming rich. Their high cost may be robbing you of your ability to accumulate real wealth.

To be very clear as to what constitutes wealth, in this book being rich means having $2,000,000 or more in liquid investments (also called liquid assets or liquid securities). What are liquid investments? Cash, mutual funds, annuities, stocks and bonds, and the cash value of your life insurance. Those investments are liquid, meaning you can sell them for cash any day, if needed. They can be left to grow or they can generate income or they can be cashed in and used for other opportunities. In some cases, profitable real estate, such as apartment houses or commercial/office buildings that have a high positive net cash flow (profit) of 20% or more and a high equity (current value less all mortgages) of 50% or more, can be considered liquid assets. Also, a wholly owned (no partners) and very profitable business can be included.

Excluded from this definition of wealth are homes, automobiles, and yachts; all nonprofitable or only slightly profitable income property; and all marginal (no-profit) or low-profit businesses. Marginal or low-profit businesses and real estate you own may become highly profitable sometime in the future, but they are not liquid and cannot be counted as part of your liquid assets now. You may also own cars and yachts and other luxuries, but don't apply them toward your $2,000,000 in liquid assets.

Why $2,000,000? Because $2,000,000 invested in AAA (triple-A) bonds, the highest rated and safest bonds, at 6.0%—a conservative figure—yields a net income of $120,000 per year. That's $10,000 per month. If you earn $10,000 a month today from your safest, most liquid investments, you can live very well. That is what "being rich" is, the ability to live well.

How Some Have Become Rich by Choice

Here are four stories showing how ordinary people built their wealth and became rich. The stories are based on real people and their choices, although names and other details have been changed.

Sandy

Sandy was 22 years old when she graduated from college and landed her first job. Since her family didn't have much money and never would, she knew she had to start investing for herself if she ever expected to have anything. Nobody was going to do it for her. So Sandy made one big choice: She put $2,000 into an individual retirement account (IRA). Then she chose to do the same every year after that. No matter what else she was doing, she always put $2,000 into her IRA.

A few years later, she was married. She and her husband had three children, bought a house, and did the things all families do. Yet every year she managed to put $2,000 either into her own spousal IRA (for nonworking spouses) or into her husband's IRA. Then her husband died at 48 and she had to go back to work. She still continued putting $2,000 a year into her IRA. She had an average rate of return on her money of 12%, which is what the U.S. stock market has averaged for the last 75 years.[1] Some years it gained more and some years it lost money, but it averaged 12%. Sandy is 58 now. At age 60 she will have approximately $1,300,000 in her IRA account, combined with her deceased husband's, and she can retire if she wants to. If

1. Ibbotson Associates, Chicago, Illinois, www.ibbotson.com.

she works to age 65 and continues to contribute to her IRA and lets it grow, she could have over $2,000,000 in her IRA account.

Bill and Pat

Bill was 30 years old and had never saved a dime. He lived well, loved life, and spent every dollar he earned. He had a good job and a good income, and he and his wife were expecting their first baby. At that point, he started thinking, and he and his wife, Pat, had a long talk. Then, instead of buying the new car he wanted, which would have cost about $250 a month, they made some new choices. They decided he could drive his present car for a few more years and put the $250 a month he would save into his company's new tax-qualified 401(k) retirement plan. If he continues investing $250 a month and averages 12% per year on his investment, he will have at least $1,400,000 in his account at age 65. If his employer contributes any matching funds at all to the 401(k) plan, he will have much more. If his employer matches 50% of its employees' contributions, which is common, Bill will have $2,100,000 just in that one account.

Charles and Cindy

At age 40, Charles and his wife, Cindy, decided to take stock of their lives and see what their financial future looked like. They had $6,000 in their checking account, $3,500 in a small savings account, and $7,500 in a mutual fund. They also had a home, only partly paid for, two cars in good condition, and two children ready for college. They decided that they needed to make a lot of tough choices if they were going to be able to help their children through college and also be able to retire someday.

After looking at their present situation, they made some new choices. Charles immediately started putting 6% of his salary into his company's 401(k) plan, and he and his wife also started adding at least $150 a month to their mutual fund. He was earning about $60,000 a year, so 6% of his income came to $3,600 per year. His $150 a month was another $1,800 a year. If all goes well and the returns on their investment stay in the range of 12% a year, Charles will have about $535,000 in his 401(k) plan when he is ready to retire at 65, plus the amount of any matching contributions from the company he works for. Charles and Cindy could have $265,000 in their mutual fund account, less the taxes they will have to pay on gains in their fund account each year and less what they take out to use for their children's college educations. This could leave them as much as $800,000, which is enough to retire on. There are many more steps they could take. For example, they are investing only 9%

of their income—$3,600 + $1,800 = $5,400, which is 9% of $60,000. They could invest more and probably will when their children finish college.

Dr. Dave

Dr. Dave had just been divorced and was starting over financially. His ex-wife had the house, the children, and most of the money. She received child support and alimony every month. Dave had his medical practice, which was a good one. He was 45 years old and made over $300,000 a year. Out of that he paid his nurse, receptionist, two part-time accounting staffers, his office rent, alimony, child support, and more. He needed to build his wealth fast if he was going to retire by the time he was 60, as he had always planned.

Dr. Dave had $60,000 left in his half of his Keogh plan (a qualified retirement plan for small businesses) and $20,000 in his checking account, which he needed to run his office. That's all he had left. After talking with his certified public accountant (CPA), his certified financial planner (CFP), and his lawyer, he chose new financial goals and began to implement his plan to achieve them. He set up a new qualified retirement plan for his office that allowed employee contributions in addition to employer contributions (Salary Reduction–Simplified Employee Pension Plan, or SAR-SEP), contributed $1,500 a month for himself, and contributed for his two full-time employees. He also bought a high-cash-value life insurance policy for himself that cost $30,000 a year. This didn't leave him much spending money, but the plan he developed with his advisors would build him a fine estate by age 60 and even more by 65. The figures came to approximately $750,000 in the SAR-SEP and $740,000 in the insurance policy at age 60 and approximately $1,452,500 and $1,172,000, respectively, at 65. In addition, upon retirement he could probably sell his practice for another $600,000, based on today's dollars.

You Can Do It Too

These four stories are based on true situations. Any one could be your story. These people looked at their lives and decided it was time to make some changes. They had to make new choices, and they did. They adopted a new attitude, saying "I need to do what's best for me and my family" and "I need to take care of myself, I need to start building my future."

These people chose to make the changes necessary to start building their own wealth. With a changed attitude, they set new goals: Build toward retirement and wealth now; buy a new car later. Stop spending; start building. They told themselves,

"Let's look ahead and see where we want to end up. If we want to be rich and retired in 25 years, then let's choose a path that will take us there."

All of these people already have, or soon will, become rich. They all have the right attitudes and have made riches a goal. They know the process will take time but not too much time. They either have reached their goal or will reach it by age 65. Average life expectancy is now about 87 years of age in the United States. Since these people all plan to retire by age 65, they will be retired and *rich* for an average of 22 years—about one-quarter of their lifetimes. And if they teach their children how to live well and be rich, they and their families can be rich forever.

Of course, all of these people will have problems and face challenges as they go along, but these will be similar to the problems and challenges they would have had even if they hadn't chosen to become rich. Being rich doesn't mean they won't face challenges and have problems to solve. We all have those; they're part of life! But these people will have problems *and* be rich, and they will have the last laugh.

Chapter 2
The Basics: Numbers, Forms, and How to Start

Before we go any further, we need to look at some numbers. Sandy, Bill and Pat, Charles and Cindy, and Dr. Dave got rich because of the numbers. We will explain all the steps of the financial planning process starting in the next chapter, but first let's look at the amount of money you have available to invest now, the rate of return you expect, and the number of years you will be investing.

Let's say you have $10,000 that you can spend any way you want to—a new car, a down payment on a house, a college fund, remodeling, a vacation, sports equipment, a boat.

What if you invested the money so you would be *rich* someday? What would the results be?

- $10,000 invested at 12% for 20 years becomes $96,500
- After 30 years it becomes $300,00
- After 40 years it becomes $930,000

Wouldn't that $300,000 look and feel better in 30 years than that new car you wanted? After 40 years, your $10,000 is almost $1,000,000!

The numbers indicate that you can become rich if:

- You have a steady income
- You have 20, 30, or 40 years until your retirement or the age at which you wish to be rich
- You are ready to start *now* to put money into your investment plan

The numbers also indicate that you won't become rich if:

- You don't start now
- You choose not to add to your investment account regularly, i.e., weekly, biweekly, or monthly
- You take money out of your "I Choose to Be Rich" account from time to time for current expenses

Table 2.1   Results of Investing at 12% until Age 65

Amount Invested	Age You Begin Investing								
	Age 18	Age 20	Age 25	Age 30	Age 35	Age 40	Age 45	Age 50	Age 55
$5 per week $260 per year	$496,600	$395,460	$233,340	$125,580	$70,200	$38,740	$20,980	$10,840	$5,100
$25 per week $1,300 per year	2,483,000	1,977,300	1,116,700	627,900	351,000	193,700	104,910	54,210	25,540
$38 per week $1,976 per year	3,724,160	3,005,490	1,697,380	954,400	533,520	294,420	159,460	82,400	38,820
$50 per month $600 per year	1,146,000	912,600	515,400	289,800	162,000	89,400	48,420	25,020	11,790
$166 per month $1,992 per year	3,804,720	3,029,830	1,711,128	962,130	537,840	206,800	160,750	83,060	39,140

The Numbers

Table 2.1 shows amounts invested at 12% interest, which has been the average gain in the U.S. stock market over the last 75 years. Here's how to use this table:

1. Circle the age closest to your present age at the top of the table. Choose an amount in the left column—say, $5 per week. Read across the row labeled "$5 per week" until you come to the column under your age. For example, if you are 35 years old and you choose $5 per week, you would come to $70,200. That's the amount you can have at age 65.

2. Circle the amount of money you can have at 65.
   - If you plan to invest $10 per week, double the total.
   - If you plan to invest $15 per week, triple it.
   - If you plan to invest $20 per week, quadruple it.

The numbers show that *you* can be rich. For example, $10 per week invested at an average 12% becomes $41,900 in 20 years or $140,500 in 30 years. Or $100 per month invested at an average 12% becomes $96,800 in 20 years or $324,300 in 30 years.

If you were able to earn 20% per year, as many have done, then your $10 per week could grow to $133,000 or $988,000 and your $100 per month could grow to $310,000 or $2,297,000 in 20 or 30 years.

But first you have to start. Like Charles and Cindy did at age 40, you have to take a look at where you are now. This is where you start—right here, right now.

By the end of this book, if you choose to, you will have a complete, accurate, and detailed financial picture of where you are now. You will also have the tools you need to chart your course to riches, to real wealth. And if you choose to, you will become wealthy. The choice is yours.

Forms

The first step is to get a detailed picture of your income, both annually and monthly. You also need a rough idea of the assets you own or are buying now. Get a pencil and keep it with you as you read this book. Four simple forms are presented in this book for you to fill in. Make at least two copies of each one as you will use them several times, at least once a year.

Form 1—Income

The first form, Form 1, is to be used to list all of your income. This information is not for the Internal Revenue Service (IRS); it's strictly for you.

Form 1　　　　Income

Your total income consists of the following items:

	Weekly or Monthly	Annually
1. Your *gross* salary, wages, commission, and tips from your job	$ _____	$ _____
2. Your spouse's wages, salary, commission, and tips	_____	_____
3. Income from your second job	_____	_____
4. Income from your spouse's second job	_____	_____
5. Interest earned from savings accounts, CDs, money market accounts	_____	_____
6. Interest earned in annuities	_____	_____
7. Interest earned in cash-value life insurance	_____	_____
8. Interest earned from bonds and bond funds	_____	_____
9. Tax-free interest from municipal bonds and bond funds	_____	_____

	Weekly or Monthly	**Annually**
10. Dividends from stocks, mutual funds, and variable annuities	_____	_____
11. Rents from income property	_____	_____
12. Royalties	_____	_____
13. Pensions	_____	_____
14. Social Security	_____	_____
15. Other (specify: _____)	_____	_____
16. Other (specify: _____)	_____	_____
Totals	$ _____	$ _____

These totals are your most important statistics—they're your total income. Your income is what you use to build wealth; therefore, your figures must be accurate.

Your Income

You must be constantly aware of three facts about your income:

1. Your income is your most important asset. It is what you use to build your wealth. It needs to be preserved and protected, and that means you'll need disability income insurance.

2. Your income should be increased and built up in every way possible. You may not be able to affect your income in big ways, but every little bit helps, and over a long time it helps a lot. If you are paid a salary and work a steady 40-hour week without added pay for overtime, you can't do much to increase your income except to do your job well and look for raises and promotions from time to time. If you can get overtime pay, take it whenever it's offered and add the extra income to your wealth-building plan.

3. Overtime pay is extra income, the income that will make you rich. Don't spend all of your extra income. Invest at least half of it to build your wealth. It is *extra;* you should live on your regular income.

Your Extra Income

You don't think you have extra income? What about the interest income from your savings accounts, money market accounts, annuities, and mutual funds? This investment income must be reinvested. You can choose to reinvest it in the account in which it was earned. Or you can choose to send all the dribs and drabs of small miscellaneous income checks you get to one account—a mutual fund money market account would be a good choice. As cash builds up there, you can add it to your existing investments or use it for new ones. And remember, this is *extra* income. This is not the money you use for your regular IRA contributions or other planned investments. This is extra income, and it will help to make you rich.

You generally have a choice about where to put your money, whether in a bank account, an annuity, or a mutual fund. In most cases, you should choose the highest rate of return available in each of these types of investments. The only reason not to take the highest rate of return is if there is a question of safety, a difference in risk. You want your account to grow—you have a goal to reach—so you want the highest return you can get with safety.

For example, as this is written, money market accounts at banks in California pay from 1.0 to 2.0%. The same kind of account at a mutual fund pays from 4.0 to 6.0%. Which do you choose? It's a little more work to open a money market account at a mutual fund, but it pays more and therefore you earn more.

Let's say you keep about $3,000 in your money market account as a cash reserve and for small emergencies. Your bank pays 2.0% and your mutual fund company pays 5.0%.

$3,000 at 2% interest = $3,000 × .02 = $60/year; $60/12 = $5/month

$3,000 at 5% interest = $3,000 × .05 = $150/year; $150/12 = $12.50/month

The difference in interest is only $7.50 per month, but it is $90 per year. That $90 is extra income. How will you use it?

Table 2.2   The Growth of Savings at Different Interest Rates over 20 Years

Initial Savings	Interest Rate				
	2%	**3%**	**4%**	**5%**	**6%**
$1,000	$1,486	$1,806	$2,191	$2,653	$3,207
$3,000	4,458	5,418	6,573	7,959	9,621
$5,000	7,430	9,030	10,955	13,265	16,035
$10,000	14,860	18,060	21,910	26,530	32,070

Over 20 years, $1,000 at 2% interest grows to $1,486. At 6%, $1,000 grows to $3,207. Notice that at a 2% interest rate over 20 years, your money grows by less than 50%. At 4%, it more than doubles, and at 6%, it more than triples.

For a full year, the difference in interest earned in the example above is only $90 ($7.50 × 12 = $90), not a lot. But watch what happens over 20 years: 20 × $90 = $1,800; 5% interest on $1,800 equals another $1,123, for a total of $3,123. If you have $6,000 in your money market, the difference will be $6,246. This is substantial; it is worth the extra effort to earn the additional $3,123 or $6,246. This extra money is the result of the *choices* you make. You do not have to *work* for it, just make a better choice. During your working years, all these choices will bring you hundreds of thousands of dollars of additional income, the income you need to become wealthy.

Now study your income on Form 1 and see if there are any areas where you can increase your income. Make notes in the margin about any ideas you get. Don't let them slip away, forgotten. Study the form carefully. It will help determine your future and your wealth. Ask yourself these questions:

- Are there any areas where you have *no* income but you could have some? Do you have too much cash in your checking account, that is, more than you normally spend in one month? If so, could some of it be put in a money market fund or other investment?
- Do you have money in mutual funds that pay only 5–8% when you could be in funds that pay 10–15% or more?
- Are you thinking about taking a better job?
- Should you take classes to learn extra skills that will earn you more pay?
- Could you work a few hours a week at a second job?
- Do you have an old car that is *not* used that could be sold and the money invested?
- Do you have any household or personal items (assets, collections, stuff, junk) that could be sold and turned into additional investments and extra income?

Study your savings and investments at least once a year to see if you can earn more. Take Form 1 out every year and study it and bring it up to date. Do this the first week in January, when you start compiling your tax information.

Here are some tips for increasing your income:

- Banks are competitive; use the ones that pay higher interest on your checking and savings accounts.
- Use credit unions. They usually pay higher interest than banks.
- Continually review and upgrade all your investment accounts to make sure they're competitive.
- Take your money out of mutual funds that are not doing well and put it in funds that are doing very well. It's your money, and you deserve to get the best deal available for your money.

Form 2—Assets

The next information needed is your assets, that is, what you own. Use Form 2 to list your assets.

Form 2   Assets

(Leave blank to be filled in later)	Assets	No. of Items	Current Value	(Figure Here)
___ ___	Cash	___	$ _____	
___ ___	Checking accounts	___	_____	
___ ___	Money market accounts	___	_____	
___ ___	Home	___	_____	
___ ___	Second home	___	_____	
___ ___	Rental property	___	_____	
___ ___	Business(es)	___	_____	
___ ___	Stocks	___	_____	
___ ___	Bonds	___	_____	
___ ___	Mutual funds	___	_____	
___ ___	Annuities, fixed	___	_____	
___ ___	Annuities, variable	___	_____	
___ ___	IRAs	___	_____	
___ ___	401(k)s	___	_____	
___ ___	Profit-sharing plans	___	_____	
___ ___	403(b)	___	_____	

(Leave blank to be filled in later)	Assets	No. of Items	Current Value	(Figure Here)
____ ____	Other retirement plans	_____	_____	
____ ____	Savings accounts	_____	_____	
____ ____	Cash value of life insurance	_____	_____	
____ ____	Automobiles	_____	_____	
____ ____	Boats	_____	_____	
____ ____	Trailers	_____	_____	
____ ____	Motorhomes	_____	_____	
____ ____	Other vehicles, planes	_____	_____	
____ ____	Collections: art, jewelry, antiques, tools, paintings, weapons, etc.	_____	_____	
____ ____	Cameras	_____	_____	
____ ____	Coins	_____	_____	
____ ____	Other	_____	_____	
____ ____	Personal property, furniture, televisions, stereos, etc.	_____	_____	
____ ____	Miscellaneous	_____	_____	
	Total	_____	$ _____	

Here's how to use the form: If you own two businesses, write "2" in the "No. of Items" column and their total value in the "Current Value" column. If you own eight stocks, write "8" and their total value, and so on. Ignore any debt on this form. Write in the current market value of your cars, your home, your income property. You need to get a clear picture of what you *own* and its current value.

Your assets are everything you own or are buying. Look at your list on Form 2 and study it for a while. Consider these questions:

- Are these the assets you want to own—your home, vehicles, collections, stocks, mutual funds, and so on? If not, why do you own them?
- Are they good values now?
- Will they be good values in the future?
- Can you afford the payments, or should you sell an asset that costs too much each month and invest the amount of the monthly payment in your wealth-building plan?
- Should you convert or exchange one asset type for another? For example, should you sell treasury bonds earning 4.75% and buy a growth mutual fund?
- Do these assets generate the high rate of dividends or interest or capital gains or profits you need and expect?
- Could you do better?
- Do these assets fit into your wealth-building plan? Will they make you rich?
- Will you want these assets when you become rich? Why or why not?

These are the assets you have bought with the money you have had so far. How do you like the list? Whatever your answer, the list constantly needs to be upgraded, expanded, and built up. If you have only a house, a car, and one mutual fund, keep adding to that fund if it is a good one. That one fund can make you rich.

Your assets are your present-day wealth. Some, such as motorhomes, cost money to maintain, so they are expenses. Are those expenses worth it? Could you sell or exchange an "expensive to maintain" asset for another that is not so expensive to maintain?

Some of these assets, such as IRAs and mutual funds, will generate the income you need for your retirement. They can also be the basis for your family's wealth, as they can be passed on to the next generation.

In chapters 5, 11, 12, and 13, we will look at how you select, purchase, finance, refinance, and pay off these assets. Right now, you just need to be aware of them—what they are, why you bought them, whether they are working for you or not, and how to make them grow.

Now You Can Begin

Since these assets are your wealth today, this is where you begin. You now have what you need to get started on your plan to be rich:

- A new attitude
- A willingness to make new choices
- A desire to be rich
- A goal of $2,000,000 (or some other number) in liquid securities
- An income stream that you can use to satisfy your desire for real wealth
- A growing list of assets

In the rest of this book, you will learn how to make the right choices every day so that you will become rich.

Chapter 3
The Seven Steps in
the Financial Planning Process

Financial planning is a lifelong process—one you should choose to start now. Every month that you delay will cost you thousands of dollars later. (You'll learn why in chapter 7.) Starting now does not finish the process, however; it is only the beginning. The process will continue over your lifetime, and you can teach it to your children so that it lasts over their lifetimes, too, generation after generation.

The financial planning process is simple and highly effective, and it consists of just seven steps. As you work through these seven steps, keep these items in mind: ownership taxes, inflation, and compound interest. They are the keys to financial success and riches and will be covered in detail in following chapters.

The Seven Steps

The seven steps in the financial planning process are as follows:

1. Establish cash reserves
2. Manage risk with insurance
3. Have guaranteed savings
4. Invest for growth
5. Plan for taxes
6. Plan for retirement
7. Plan for your estate

Let's look briefly at each of these. You may be taking some of these steps already. (Remember that the process takes place over time. It could be 20 or 30 years after starting the process before you plan your retirement in detail and even longer before you prepare an estate plan.)

Step 1—Establish Cash Reserves

You must have a cash reserve, however small, before you can do anything else. Cash reserves are the dollars you have available for immediate needs and small emergencies, and they consist of your checking accounts, passbook savings accounts, and money market accounts. You should have enough cash reserves to cover *two to three months' normal expenses* when you are working. If you were to lose your job, you could live for two to three months while looking for a new job before you'd have to start cashing in your investments, looking for additional money, or making significant changes in your lifestyle. Most people like to have three to six months' expenses in cash reserves when they are retired. It seems to add to their sense of security.

Step 2—Manage Risk with Insurance

Risk management and insurance refer to the insurance policies you need to fill the gap between what an accident, illness, or death might cost and what you can afford to pay out of your pocket for that unexpected event. You have many risks to manage; therefore, you need many kinds of insurance, including auto, health, homeowner's (if you own a home or condominium), disability, life, and long-term care insurance. Your need for insurance and the kinds to buy are discussed in chapter 13.

Step 3—Have Guaranteed Savings

Savings are not investments, they are savings—fixed rate, low rate, but guaranteed. Savings will not make you rich, *ever*. Guaranteed savings are dollars lent at a fixed rate of interest to big institutions that then pay you interest on your money. The money you lend to banks is called "savings" and is "deposited" in savings accounts or CDs (certificates of deposit) that are guaranteed by the U.S. government up to $100,000. The money you lend to life insurance companies goes into annuities, which are guaranteed by the insurance companies.

Your loans to the U.S. government become treasury bills (T-bills), government or U.S. Treasury bonds, and GNMA (Government National Mortgage Association, nicknamed "Ginnie Mae," a government lending agency) certificates. U.S. Treasury securities are guaranteed since they are backed by the full faith and credit of the U.S. government. GNMA buys home mortgages from banks and other lending institutions, packages them into pools of mortgages, and resells these pools to the public in blocks of $100,000 or more. GNMA certificates are guaranteed by Congress but not by the U.S. Treasury. These investments can be taxable or tax-deferred. (Tax-deferred investments would include those in IRAs and annuities.)

In addition, a wide range of corporate bonds are issued by U.S. corporations, and tax-free municipal bonds are issued by state and local governments. These bonds are not guaranteed but are backed by the assets of the corporations and governments that issue them.

The various guaranteed and nonguaranteed savings accounts and bonds currently pay from 2.5% to 9% interest. The guaranteed bonds pay less than the nonguaranteed ones since there's less risk to the investor. Therefore, if you plan to be rich, you shouldn't choose to keep much of your money in guaranteed bonds. However, for a sense of safety and to keep some money absolutely risk-free, use a guaranteed savings account.

Step 4—Invest for Growth

Growth investments are dollars invested in ownership of property, businesses, stocks, or natural resources (e.g., gold, oil, lumber) that can increase—or decrease— in value. Mutual funds are the most common form of stock and bond portfolios. They include a wide variety of investment strategies with names such as Large Cap, Small Cap, Aggressive Growth, Value, and International. Because stock mutual fund investments have averaged 12% a year over time, and managed portfolios can do much better than that, this is where you should invest most of your money.

Step 5—Plan for Taxes

Tax planning is the *deliberate* arrangement of your financial affairs to legally reduce your taxes as much as possible while you are building your wealth. Tax *evasion* is a crime. Tax *planning* can save you thousands of dollars and will build your wealth faster.

Step 6—Plan for Retirement

Retirement planning is also necessary. Like any other goal, retirement can be planned for and achieved. If you follow steps 1 through 5 well, you will be able to retire in comfort. There is no age limit. You can retire at 45, 55, or 65—sooner if you plan well, later if you don't.

Step 7—Plan for Your Estate

Estate planning is the process of planning the passage of your possessions and wealth to your chosen heirs—and no one else—with minimal estate taxes, expense, and delay. You also want to be sure that your heirs will appreciate their inheritance, enjoy it, and build on it. When you are rich, you will want your heirs to respect and care for the riches you have created, to use them well, and to continue the process of building family wealth. Being rich can be and should be a natural part of your enjoyment and experience of life.

These are the seven basic steps of financial planning. Most people use some of them without realizing it and can do fairly well. Others, like Bill, whom we met in chapter 1, suddenly discover that they need to develop a financial plan if they are ever going to take care of their responsibilities.

Bill and Pat Start to Plan

Recall that Bill was 30 and that he and his wife, Pat, were expecting their first child when they decided it was time to take charge of their finances. He was earning $40,000 a year, his wife had just stopped working, and his first step was to start putting $250 a month into his company's 401(k) plan. Then he decided he needed a house for his wife and child. How could he proceed to do everything he needed to do? Suddenly he wished he were rich, that he had a lot of money to solve all his problems. He had a good job and a good future ahead of him, so he sought advice on how to get started toward his goals.

Bill found a certified financial planner who was highly recommended by his CPA, and they sat down together. He told the planner he needed a home and a retirement plan and he wanted to be rich. The planner nodded and began taking notes. This is the plan they worked out together.

Bill and Pat's first priority was to buy a house, and for that they needed a down payment. Bill talked to his dad, who agreed to lend Bill $10,000 if he could save $10,000. That would give him $20,000 for a down payment.

How could Bill and Pat save $10,000? And how fast could they do it?

They had been renting a very nice condominium at the beach. They found they could rent a nice two-bedroom apartment away from the beach and save $200 a month. The apartment was also closer to Bill's work. In addition, as Pat had stopped working, Bill decided to claim two dependents instead of one on his tax withholding form (W-4). That gave Bill another $50 a month of take-home pay. Here were savings of $250 a month.

This was a good start. If they saved $250 a month, that would be $3,000 a year and they would have $10,000 in 40 months, a little over three years. In addition, they agreed that they could eat out less often and they could shop a little less; they could then save even more. They were excited about beginning to build their future and owning their own home.

Then their financial planner told them about compound interest. He showed them that if they saved $250 a month and earned 5% interest, paid monthly in a good money market fund, they would have $10,000 in just under 36 months, not 40 months. The magic of compound interest saved them four months—10% of their time! With this news, they gave notice at the condo, rented the apartment, and moved in at the end of the month. They were on their way.

Their Seven-Step Plan

Here is the seven-step financial plan Bill and Pat developed with their planner.

1. Cash reserves: They put the additional $250 per month into a money market mutual fund they could write checks on for emergencies. This money would grow to $10,000 in less than three years if they didn't write any checks.

2. Risk management and insurance: They already had auto insurance and health and disability insurance through Bill's employer. Now that they were going to have a baby and buy a house, Bill needed life insurance. He took out a $150,000 universal life policy with cash value buildup. It cost them about $58 a month, which they had to squeeze out of their budget, but it was worth it. Part of the monthly premium they paid went into a savings account within the life insurance policy. This is the cash value of the policy, and it grows, tax-deferred, every year. They planned that the policy would be paid up at age 65 and the cash value could then add to their retirement income. Also, they wouldn't be paying life insurance premiums when they were retired.

3. Guaranteed savings: At this point, they had only their cash reserves. After they had about $2,000 in cash reserves, they would start a tax-free bond fund. This would pay higher interest than the money market fund and help keep their taxes down.

   They would also start to build guaranteed savings in Bill's universal life policy but not until they had owned it for two years.

4. Growth dollars: Here they had Bill's 401(k) plan working for them. He was contributing $250 a month from his pay. This amount was tax-free, as his contribution was made before the company deducted taxes from his wages. The earnings in the plan were tax-deferred *and* his company matched his contribution with 50 cents for every dollar he put in. Because this was a long-term investment, he put 100% of his contribution into a long-term growth fund, one of the five choices the company offered. In total, Bill put $375 ($250 + $125 company match) into a growth account every month.

5. Tax planning: Suddenly, Bill and Pat had two tax benefits they never had before, with two more on the way.
   - Their 401(k) is a *big* tax-saving device, about the best you can have. Bill's contributions to the plan are not taxed as income, and the investment earnings of the plan are tax-deferred, that is, not taxed while he is working and the plan is growing.
   - The cash-value buildup of Bill's life insurance policy is also tax-free. He needs the insurance, and the cash value is a guaranteed savings account that he also needs. Being tax-free is an added benefit of the policy.
   - Their tax-free bond fund will save taxes when they start it.
   - When they buy their house in three years, the mortgage interest is a deductible expense and will save taxes.
6. Retirement planning: Bill's 401(k) is the base here as it is specifically designed for retirement. The cash value in Bill's life insurance policy will also be available during his retirement. Since Bill and Pat will buy a house with a 30-year mortgage when Bill is 33, that mortgage will be paid off when he is 63, so they won't have any mortgage payments during their retirement. They will be able to live on less income.
7. Estate planning: Bill now has a life insurance policy with Pat as his beneficiary. It is big enough to pay off almost all of the mortgage on their new home, so if Bill were to die, Pat could live there with their children with little or no mortgage expense. She is also beneficiary of Bill's 401(k) plan. That's all they need now.

Bill and Pat are on a crash program because their first baby is on the way. The program includes a fund for a house and a retirement plan. Bill also has a life insurance policy because his family will need the policy's proceeds if he dies. (He didn't need it before he had children.) He and Pat have a new attitude and they are making all the right choices. They are on their way to becoming rich.

Where they had no financial plan before and were not making any progress financially, they now have three separate financial accounts growing and working for them:

1. Bill's 401(k) plan. They owned their car (ownership is important) and decided to put what they would have spent on payments for a new car into the retirement plan: $250 + $125 (company match) = $375 per month.
2. Their joint money market account (cash reserves): $250 per month.
3. Bill's life insurance policy. The policy has a face value of $150,000; its cash value will grow by approximately $60 per month after the first two years.

This is how wealth is built. With a change in attitude, handling money, building accounts, and preparing for the future suddenly become easy and desirable. There are as many variations of this story as there are young couples.

Part 2
The Four Keys to Building Wealth

Wealth comes from your investments, and the four keys discussed in the next four chapters can help you choose the investments that will work for you. Using these keys will improve your investment results.

Chapter 4
Ownership: One Key to Riches

One key to wealth is ownership. When you own something, it's yours. You bought and paid for it. You must need it or you wouldn't have bought it. You use it. You care for it. You clean it, maintain it, repair it. If it's a stock or mutual fund, you keep a record of it. You must own things, have assets, if you are going to be rich. There is satisfaction in ownership and becoming rich. If there wasn't, why would you be doing it?

Earlier, we told the story of Bill and Pat, who were expecting their first baby. They decided that rather than buy a new car, Bill would drive the old one that they already owned for a couple more years. This freed up $250 a month that they could either invest or use for expenses for the baby. Because they owned their car, they had a choice.

If you are planning to be rich, then you will own a lot of cash, stocks, and mutual funds and maybe your business and some rental property. These investment assets must be given the same care and respect as your other assets, such as your car. The only difference is that you keep adding to your investments and you expect them to grow in value.

Owning something means it doesn't cost you anything to have. You may have to make repairs on what you own, but it's yours and you can use it for the rest of its useful life. Certainly, when you are retired, you don't want to be paying for housing. You will want the security of owning your home, free and clear. When you invest in a business, whether by buying stock or actually operating a business, you want to own it. It's okay to rent a house or apartment for a few years while you are getting started, and it's okay to lease equipment, including vehicles, for a business for a short time. And if the equipment or vehicles will quickly become obsolete, then leasing may be better than owning. But any successful manufacturing company owns its plants and grounds and equipment. Many successful professionals own their office buildings, clinics, or studios. Over the course of your lifetime, your costs go way down with ownership. The tax benefits due to depreciation are another advantage. (We'll discuss depreciation in chapter 5.)

We looked at Charles and his wife when he was 40. They bought their house for $200,000 when he was 32. Owning their own home gave them huge tax advantages because they could deduct the interest they paid on their mortgage each year. Their home also was an asset that increased in value with inflation. And finally, because they owned it, after 30 years it will be paid for, so during their retirement they won't have any more payments to make for their housing. Their housing will be free, except for insurance, taxes, and maintenance. Their friend Jerry, however, never bought a house. He lives comfortably and carefree in his apartment. After 30 years he will still be paying rent and have nothing to show for his 30 years of rent payments, except a drawer full of canceled checks.

Owning Stocks and Bonds

The money you save on taxes because you own your house, your car, or your business can be put to work in two ways. You can either invest this money in stocks and thus own shares of other people's businesses or you can loan it to banks, corporations, municipalities, or the U.S. Treasury. For these loans, you receive in exchange certificates of deposit, corporate bonds, municipal bonds, and treasury bills and bonds. These bonds are all loans and are not truly a form of ownership. The bank or other entity agrees to pay you interest at a certain rate and to pay back the loan (return your principal to you) at a certain time. As long as inflation is occurring, such fixed-rate loans are probably poor investments because they represent a fixed return of money, and money goes down in value during inflation. On the other hand, stocks tend to go up in value and keep up with inflation. Stocks are another asset you can own. If you are going to become rich, you need to own stocks, as well as businesses, real estate, and other assets.

Mutual funds that own stocks are an excellent long-term investment. The fund managers are watching their stocks, the economy, business trends, and new innovations every day. You just have to check the progress of your funds from time to time; quarterly or monthly is usually sufficient. The average rate of return in the U.S. stock market has been 12% since 1926. It was even higher the ten years from 1990 to 2000, then it came down sharply the last two months of 2000 and the first quarter of 2001.

I have clients who drive cars that are 10, 15, even 20 years old. Their cars are becoming classics and they don't cost a cent to own. These clients have license, maintenance, and insurance costs just as they would for any car, but their cars were paid for long ago. And their license and insurance costs go *down* every year because their cars are older.

If you are really planning to be rich, you must own things and you must take care of what you own. How you take care of what you have says a lot about you. It is also, according to philosopher Eric Hoffer, a sign of how civilized you are.[2] Those who take care of their houses, cars, and other possessions are civilized and therefore fit into their communities much better than those who don't.

If you are going to be rich and live well, you will fit into your neighborhood. When you own your home and you keep it up, the value of your house and the neighboring houses goes up. You look good and so does your property. The grass is cut and the landscaping is cared for. It looks prosperous. When you see a house that is run-down and its lawn is dried out and uncut, you assume the owners are poor, not rich.

Rich does not mean gaudy but well maintained and cared for. Possessions that are well maintained last longer, cost less in the long run, and are probably worth more than those that are not cared for. Run-down houses that are sold at a discount as fixer-uppers often cost more by the time they are repaired and back in good condition than well-cared-for homes. If the roof never leaks, then the plaster may never crack and crumble and the floors may never buckle. These would be expensive repairs. Houses that are well cared for need very little structural repair.

The same is also true of automobiles. Cars that are driven with care, given regular maintenance, and repaired as needed can last for years and years. Those extra years without payments are years with extra money in your pocket, available for other purchases. This can be the money you need for your personal investments.

A neighbor's wife has a 30-year-old Ford Mustang that she bought new for $2,600. She drives it every day—it still looks good and runs well—and it's worth at least $20,000 today. She has had no car payments in the last 27 years (she paid for the Mustang over three years). Think how much she could have spent on lease payments over the last 27 years or in new car payments if she had wanted a new model every few years.

With ownership also comes pride and satisfaction. There can be real comfort in your longtime possessions, just like a pair of old shoes that always feel good when you wear them. By caring for your possessions and not replacing them often, or at least not until you really needed to, you can become rich. And you can help your children keep and cherish your values and riches by passing on to them what you own. You'll find stability and serenity in having some belongings around you and your family that do not change. A favorite view out of a window, a favorite chair, an old lamp or table, heirloom dishes and silver, or an old portrait can all add to your sense of wealth and well-being.

---

2. Eric Hoffer, *Reflections on the Human Condition* (New York: Harper & Row, 1973).

Now turn back to chapter 2 and look at Form 2—Assets. This list represents what you own now. Are these items that you want to own? Do they fit in with the plan you are developing for real wealth? Do you have the right house? the right car(s)? the right investments?

You may not want, or be able, to change some of the possessions you own right now. But think about them and be aware of them. Are they what you need to achieve real wealth someday? Remember, you can have $2,000,000 in liquid assets and still live in your nice three-bedroom ranch-style house or your condo. You don't have to move.

Ownership is a key to riches, so be sure you own what you use and that the items you own are the right possessions for you—assets that increase in value over time.

Chapter 5
Inflation: Use It to Push Your Investments Faster

What makes all your assets grow? Inflation. Inflation is defined as a steady—sometimes gradual, sometimes fast—increase in prices. It makes the cost of what you buy go up year after year.

Can you use inflation? Yes, you can. During times of inflation, invest in things that go up in value and stay away from things that go down in value.

What goes up in value during inflation? Equities, stocks, real estate, commodities, lumber, fuel, food, automobiles, medical supplies, hamburgers, golf balls, professional services, hospital and hotel room costs. "Things" and "services" go up in value during inflation.

What goes down in value in times of inflation? Money. As inflation increases and prices increase, it takes more money to buy the same things. As money buys less, the value of your money decreases.

What does this tell you? Basically, put your money in "things" and take your money out of "money." "Money" in this sense means cash, checking accounts, savings accounts, and all types of bonds. Coin collections are not considered money in this sense and can be good investments because of their limited supply. They go up in value during inflation. Collections are considered things, not money.

How do you know if inflation is occurring? A simple indicator is the price of a first-class postage stamp.

- In 1970, it was 6 cents.
- In 1980, it was 15 cents.
- In 1990, it was 28 cents.
- In 1995, it was 32 cents.
- In 1998, it was 33 cents.
- In 2001, it went to 34 cents.

That's about 14% inflation per year!

Another indicator that the government gives us is the monthly CPI—consumer price index. The CPI is a measure of the average change in prices of basic consumer goods and services. It is based on the prices of clothing, shelter, transportation, doctors' and dentists' services, and other goods and services bought for day-to-day living. Inflation, as measured by the CPI, is currently 3% to 4% per year.

The government's CPI figures, however, leave out two vital elements: the price of food and the price of energy, including gasoline. These elements are included in the government's base rate of inflation but not in the CPI, the most commonly used inflation figures. They are omitted from the CPI because the government says those prices are too volatile. Such omission gives a lower, distorted view of inflation because food and gasoline are two major expenses for most people.

Houses and Inflation

In chapter 4, we mentioned Charles and Cindy and the house they bought for $200,000. Later, we will discuss the big tax advantage they receive by being able to deduct the mortgage interest every year. For now, let's look at the house from the viewpoint of inflation.

If Charles and Cindy's home cost $200,000 when they bought it and inflation averages 4% a year, that house will be worth about $648,000 in 30 years when they make their last mortgage payment, if the value of the house keeps up with inflation. Their mortgage payments will stay the same at $1,600 a month during those 30 years. They will pay about $532,800 after taxes over 30 years for a home that will be worth $648,000. If Charles gets a raise in salary from time to time, perhaps his salary will also keep up with inflation. Then he and his wife will be in the enviable position of paying for an asset that's going up in value with fixed monthly dollars that are going down in value. Every year, he'll be paying for an asset worth *more and more* with money that is worth *less and less*.

This is the perfect situation to be in and the perfect use of inflation. The same can happen with the stocks, real estate, and mutual funds you buy and own. Because Charles receives periodic salary raises, he pays a smaller percentage of his income each year for an asset that is increasing in value. The first year Charles and Cindy owned the house, they paid 48% of their income for it. In the 30th year, they will pay only 14% of their income. That's taking advantage of inflation!

Table 5.1   Effect of 4% Inflation on Wages and Fixed Mortgage Payments

In this example, the mortgage payment stays fixed at $1,600 per month, or $19,200 a year. The salary starts at $40,000 and increases 4% per year.

Year	Salary	Mortgage Payment	Mortgage as Percentage of Salary
0	$40,000	$19,200	48%
1	41,600	19,200	46
2	43,264	19,200	44
3	44,994	19,200	42
4	46,794	19,200	41
5	48,666	19,200	39
6	50,612	19,200	37
7	52,637	19,200	36
8	54,742	19,200	35
9	56,932	19,200	33
10	59,209	19,200	32
15	72,037	19,200	26
20	87,644	19,200	21
25	106,633	19,200	18
30	129,735	19,200	14

Using Inflation Three Ways

Look at this principle again. It is one of the keys to wealth in times of inflation. Three components work in your favor. Understand them, use them, and remember them.

1. Own an asset—a home, for example—that increases in value during times of inflation. The same applies to stocks and stock funds. The value of a well-run company goes up over time just because of inflation, even if the amount of business it does stays the same.

2. Because of inflation, the dollars spent on fixed-rate mortgage payments or on any long-term fixed payment plan decrease in value over time. This means that less and less purchasing power is being used to pay for an asset.

3. Because of inflation, salaries and wages tend to increase; therefore, fixed monthly payments become a smaller and smaller percentage of this larger salary. And this does not assume any promotions or job advancement, only inflation and salary increases equal to the CPI.

A Word of Caution

Any purchases of major assets during times of inflation that are financed over many years will be paid for with dollars that are declining in value—a big benefit. However, you must be aware of two factors.

The first is the finance charge. The interest on your home mortgage is tax-deductible. Interest on other purchases is not. This interest, or finance charge, adds to the cost of the item you purchase. Many credit card companies charge 18% to 29% annually, which increases the cost of your purchases substantially. In many cases, the high finance charges outweigh the increase in an asset's value due to inflation. Be aware of the interest charges before you buy. Too much interest can wipe out the value of your purchase.

The second factor to be aware of is depreciation. Depreciation is an accounting method based on the principle that any asset has a defined useful life; it wears out and loses value over time and therefore is worth less as it gets older. Homes generally are depreciated over 30 years, autos over 5 years, office equipment over 5 years, and furniture and appliances over 7 years. Depreciation is used to figure the taxable gain in value of an asset when it is sold. For example, a home bought for $200,000 and depreciated over 30 years will have a depreciated value or cost basis of $0.00 after 30 years. Land cannot be depreciated, so if part of the value of your home is the land value, that must be figured in. For simplicity here, we are ignoring the land value. If the home has gone up in value because of inflation and is then sold for $600,000, the profit on the sale, according to IRS rules and general accounting principles, is not $400,000, as you'd logically think it might be.

Table 5.2   Figuring Capital Gain

Common assumption about capital gain (excludes depreciation)		
Sale price of home	$600,000	
Purchase price	– 200,000	
Profit	$400,000	taxable, long-term capital gain
Correct calculation of capital gain (includes depreciation)		
Sale price of home	$600,000	
Depreciated cost basis	– 0	
Profit	$600,000	taxable long-term capital gain

A home normally goes up in value because of inflation, even as it is being depreciated for tax and accounting purposes. (Note: To increase in value because of inflation, a home must be well built, well maintained, and located in a well-cared-for neighborhood. Without proper maintenance or in a decaying neighborhood, it can go down in value.) Because of depreciation, you end up paying taxes on the gain in value.

Automobiles depreciate much faster than inflation can increase their value. Most of this depreciation is because of obsolescence and style changes. A 10-year-old car, properly maintained, still does everything a brand new car does; it just looks different. The same is true of television sets, refrigerators, furniture, and most of the other items you buy. They depreciate rapidly; that is, their resale value drops to almost nothing in a few years. However, if a television or anything else is well made to begin with, it can give years and years of excellent service, long after it has been paid for and has depreciated to zero resale value. And this means you get "free" use of the product while your money works—and grows—in other, beneficial ways.

Renters and Inflation

Let's look at the effect inflation has on renters or people who lease rather than buy.

Charles's friend Jerry is renting an apartment in the same neighborhood as Charles for only $1,100 a month. His landlord has raised his rent about 4% a year to keep up with inflation. The landlord's income will keep up with inflation, and Jerry, after 30 years, will be paying this smart landlord about $3,500 a month, not $1,100, for the same apartment. Jerry is paying more and more for the same thing. Where Charles's percentage of income spent on housing goes down every year, Jerry's does not. Jerry's income and rent both increase about 4% a year. In fact, if Jerry's income doesn't go up by at least 4% every year, he will be spending a greater percentage for the same apartment. In 30 years, he also will be paying a whole lot more for his housing, at $3,500 per month, than his friend Charles, who will still pay just $1,600.

Oil was $2 a barrel until 1972; now it is $24–$30 a barrel. Gold was $35 an ounce until 1971; now it is $250–$350. Stamps were 6 cents; now they are 34 cents. Cokes used to cost a nickel; now they're $1. McDonald's hamburgers used to be 19 cents; now they're 79 cents or more. Prices go up because of inflation.

Inflation is not uniform at 3% or 4% every year. Since 1945, it has been as low as 1% and as high as 13%. High inflation affects investments differently. In 1978–80, real estate values were increasing 15% a year and stocks didn't increase in value at all. Then in 1985, real estate values started decreasing and stocks were increasing at about 18% a year. However, over the longer term, 10 to 20 years, both of these investment types (assets) have increased in value.

Stocks and Inflation

When you choose to own stocks or equities, you own companies, which are things. You can own oil companies, communications companies, Internet and high-tech companies, large-cap companies (valued or capitalized at over $10 billion) or small-cap companies (valued up to $1 billion), electric utilities, computer manufacturers, chip makers, software companies, foreign and domestic companies, and any other kind of company you want, or you can own many kinds mixed together in a mutual fund. They all are available.

Stocks and stock mutual funds have grown an average of 12% a year for the last 75 years; therefore, they make an excellent investment vehicle for you as part of your long-term plan to grow rich. If you doubt this growth rate of 12% a year, go to your public library or the Internet and look at the Ibbotson Reports. These reports, issued by Ibbotson Associates, based at the University of Chicago, go back to 1926 and show conclusively that good stocks, like those in the S&P (Standard and Poor's) 500, America's 500 largest companies, have averaged over 12% a year. Then read the *Morningstar Reports* on mutual funds (an independent description and analysis of all mutual funds), also at your library and on the Internet. You will find hundreds of funds that have averaged over 12% growth for the last 10 years or more.

John D. Rockefeller, Henry Ford, Andrew Carnegie, and Andrew Mellon all built and owned their companies and became extremely rich. So did computer-industry tycoons Bill Gates, Lawrence Ellison, Marc Andressen, and Steve Case. Nobody ever became rich by just saving money in a bank. But people who invest their money in bank stock, who are in fact "owners" of the bank, like Mellon and Rockefeller, can become very rich.

Invest in companies that are doing well—for example, those that have increasing sales and profits—and as long as we have inflation, your investments will tend to increase in value. There is no guarantee of this, of course. Good companies, like those in the S&P 500, hire the best managers in the world to keep the companies growing, keep their profits high, and keep ahead of inflation. One measure of a manager's performance is how well the stock performs. Does the share price go up each year?

Note: This discussion of stocks is meant to show you the long-term benefits of owning stocks. It does not apply in the short term to many current Internet, dot-com, or other phenomenal stocks. Many of these companies' stocks rose to extraordinarily high values in late 2000, then fell as much as 80–90% in 2001. Many people who invested in these hot stocks lost a lot of money when the prices of those stocks fell. This situation also pushed down the value of stocks in all U.S. markets.

If you own a mutual fund that owns stocks, the fund's manager is working for you. Well-run companies make excellent long-term investments for two reasons. First, a well-run company does more and more business every year. If the company maintains the same percentage of profit on more business, it will have more profit. Second, because of inflation the prices a company charges for its goods and services should go up periodically. If prices go up and the company maintains the same percentage of profit, then profit will go up, too. Increased profits help drive stock prices up. Therefore, you should invest in stocks and stock funds that have averaged 12% growth in value (share price) or more per year, partly because of inflation.

Savings and Inflation

If you owned a $10,000 savings certificate of deposit (CD) that paid 6% interest, you would receive $600 in interest each year. At the end of 10 years, you would have received $6,000 in interest and still have your $10,000. How does this compare to owning a good, strong fund of dividend-paying companies? What if you invested your $10,000 in a mutual fund of such stocks that was paying a 6% dividend each year? Because of the growth mentioned above, this fund would probably keep up with inflation. If inflation was running at the rate of 4% a year, the share price and the dividend also should increase by 4% a year, on average. So this investment in dividend-paying stocks could be worth $14,800 at the end of 10 years and could have paid you almost $7,200 in dividends. Historically, this is what has happened. This type of investment takes advantage of inflation, and it could be better for you than putting all of your money in a CD.

Table 5.3   Value of a CD versus Dividend-Paying Stocks That Increase 4% a Year due to Inflation

Year	$10,000 CD	6% Interest	$10,000 Dividend-Paying Stocks	6% Dividend
1	$10,000	$600	$10,400	$600
2	10,000	600	10,816	624
3	10,000	600	11,248	648
4	10,000	600	11,698	674
5	10,000	600	12,166	701
6	10,000	600	12,653	729
7	10,000	600	13,159	759
8	10,000	600	13,685	789
9	10,000	600	14,233	821
10	10,000	600	14,802	853
	$10,000	$6,000	$14,802	$7,198

At the end of 10 years, the value of a $10,000 CD at 6% interest is still $10,000, and you have received $6,000 in interest for a total of $16,000.

At the end of 10 years, the value of a $10,000 dividend stock fund with a 6% dividend could be $14,802, and you could have received $7,198 in interest for a total of $22,000, a difference of $6,000.

Table 5.4   Current Bank Interest less Taxes and Inflation

Year	CD Rate	Maximum Federal Tax Rate	CPI Inflation Rate	Real Return (after Taxes and Inflation)
1969	7.91%	50%	6.1%	–2.14%
1970	7.65	50	5.5	– 1.67
1971	5.21	50	3.4	–0.79
1972	5.02	50	3.4	–0.89
1973	8.31	50	8.8	–4.65
1974	9.98	62	12.2	–8.41
1975	6.89	62	7.0	–4.38
1976	5.62	62	4.8	–2.66
1977	5.92	60	6.8	–4.43
1978	8.61	60	9.0	–5.56
1979	11.44	59	13.3	–8.61
1980	12.99	59	12.4	–7.07
1981	15.77	59	8.9	–2.43
1982	12.57	50	3.9	2.39
1983	9.27	48	3.8	1.02
1984	10.68	45	4.0	1.87
1985	8.24	45	3.8	0.73
1986	6.50	45	1.1	2.48
1987	7.01	33	4.4	0.05
1988	7.91	33	4.4	0.90
1989	9.08	33	4.6	1.48
1990	8.17	31	6.1	–0.46
1991	5.91	31	3.1	0.97
1992	3.76	31	2.9	–0.31
1993	3.16	31	2.7	–0.52
1994	4.96	31	2.7	0.72
1995	5.98	31	2.7	1.43
1996	5.47	31	2.7	1.07
1997	5.16	31	2.4	1.16
1998	5.46	38	2.6	0.78
1999	5.87	38	3.7	– 0.06
2000	6.18	38	2.8	1.03

If inflation is 4% or more (it was as high as 13% in 1978–80 and has often been 6% or more) and you take taxes into consideration, your fixed-rate CD will actually lose purchasing power over a period of time; therefore, don't put much of your money into fixed-rate savings.

Now go back to Form 1—Income in chapter 2 and look at each item from the standpoint of inflation. Will this income increase and keep up with the rate of inflation, or is it at a fixed rate and stuck at a low level? Put an *i* (increase) in front of each item of income that will go up with inflation.

- The interest earned on money market funds goes up and down with the general level of interest rates in the country. Put an *i* in front of your money market account.
- Annuity rates do the same—*i*.
- Long-term bank CDs (4–10 years) and bonds of all kinds (5–30 years) have fixed interest rates that do not change with inflation. This is a benefit when rates are falling but a big disadvantage when rates are rising. Don't put an *i* in front of CDs and bonds.

Now do the same using Form 2—Assets.

- Real estate tends to keep up with inflation—*i*.
- So do stocks and stock mutual funds—*i*.
- Bonds and bond funds do not.

Again, study these two lists from the point of view of current inflation and what you expect inflation to be in the future. Check these lists every year and ensure that your income in all areas will keep up with inflation and that your assets will increase in value in step with inflation. This simple process of being aware of inflation and adjusting your sources of income and your assets to keep up with, or ahead of, inflation will keep you on the road to riches.

If a week at a good resort costs $2,000 now, you plan to retire in 20 years, and inflation is 4%, that week is going to cost you $4,380 in 20 years. Are you going to want more or fewer weeks at that resort when you retire? Learn to use inflation now so you can have more weeks there when you retire.

Chapter 6
The Tax Laws: Use Them to Your Advantage

Everything you earn is yours to keep—except for what you have to pay in taxes. You do have a choice, though, as to whether you will understand and use the tax laws to your advantage in your drive to riches or ignore them and pay excess taxes. The money you save on taxes goes right into your pocket. The money spent on taxes goes to the government. You choose whom you want to pay!

You don't have to be a tax expert to use tax laws to your advantage, but from time to time you will need expert advice from a good CPA. The federal tax code is a very complicated set of laws, and lately Congress has been in the habit of adjusting and changing the tax laws every year.

All Income Is Taxable

The taxes you pay are based on your total earned income. *All* income, every penny you earn, is taxable unless Congress makes an exception. Income consists of earned wages, salaries, fees, tips, and commissions; interest and dividends; and capital gains and lottery winnings. It also consists of other income from refunds, alimony received, property rents, your business, and so on.

Some "income" items could be losses, and it is important to be aware of the fact that you can offset taxable income with allowable losses when figuring your taxes. Take advantage of this deduction when you can. It will save you money, and that means more money in *your* pocket.

Another way to reduce your taxable income is to use "adjustments" to income. These include contributions to qualified retirement plans, charitable contributions, alimony paid, one-half of the self-employment tax, and many others.

The key to using the tax laws is to learn the list of allowable deductions. In fact, make a copy of the list and keep it handy year-round so you can refer to it often and keep track of the money you spend that is deductible.

A good friend of mine spends much of his spare time in January, February, and March each year totaling up all his deductions so that he can minimize his taxes. In fact, he hardly ever owes any taxes after using all his deductions. Keeping track of your deductions is up to you. It's another choice you have to make. The money you save in taxes is yours to spend or invest. It can be instrumental in how fast you become rich.

Tax Deductions

Two major deductions are a big help in building wealth. One is the allowable deduction of interest you pay on the mortgage on your primary and secondary residences; the other is the deduction allowed for your contributions to qualified retirement plans, including IRAs, 401(k)s, 403(b)s, and Keogh plans.

IRAs

In chapter 1, I told the story of Sandy, 58, who graduated from college at 22 and invested $2,000 a year into a tax-deductible and tax-deferred IRA. She has contributed this amount every year. If she continues to do so until she is 65, she will have contributed $86,000 to her IRA over a span of 43 years. Two thousand dollars a year isn't a whole lot of money, but it is enough.

Let's examine this IRA in detail and discover what an amazing wealth builder it is just because it uses the tax laws.

Sandy started working and earned $600 a week—$31,200 a year. Using an average tax rate of 20%, she would pay $6,240 in U.S. taxes on her $31,200 income (20% is actually a little high, as most people pay less than 20% in taxes after claiming their exemptions and deductions). Without putting $2,000 into an IRA, Sandy would pay $400 in taxes on that $2,000 she earned, and she could then save or invest the remaining $1,600. If she did that for 43 years, she would invest $68,800 ($1,600 × 43), not $86,000.

Let's assume Sandy invests this $1,600 per year in mutual funds with an average return of 12% a year and has to pay taxes on that profit each year. (Note: In a mutual fund, the capital gains realized inside the fund—from the buying and selling of stocks— by law have to be paid out each year along with all interest and stock dividends received and, therefore, are taxable to fund investors.) Paying taxes at Sandy's 20% rate could reduce her long-term rate of return to 9.6% (12% - 20% of 12% = 12% - 2.4% = 9.6%).

Thus, Sandy's total return from investing $1,600 per year, earning 9.6% for 43 years, is $944,000—a very nice sum.

But since Sandy earned $2,000 and chose to invest it in her tax-deductible IRA, she did not have to pay $400 in taxes each year. The whole $2,000 was invested, not just the $1,600 left after paying taxes.

She invested $2,000 a year in a mutual fund inside her *tax-deductible and tax-deferred* IRA. Let's assume the mutual fund averages 12% over the next 43 years. Because it is tax deferred, she gets the full 12% in her account each year, not just

9.6%. And $2,000 per year earning 12% for 43 years equals *$2,420,000*—more than the $2,000,000 threshold for being rich and $1,476,000 greater than $944,000! In fact, it's more than twice as much. (She could retire earlier—her choice.)

(Note: The $2,420,000 in the IRA is taxable when money is taken out of the IRA, and a large part of the $944,000 is not. But even so, the IRA account, after taxes, amounts to significantly more than the personal account. The exact difference depends on how she takes the money out of her IRA during her retirement.)

And there is more to this IRA than that. Sandy saved an average of $400 in taxes on each contribution. That means it really cost her only $1,600 for an investment that was worth $2,000. So in investment terms, her $1,600 grew to $2,000, an increase of $400 the first year and every year she contributes. That's a 25% rate of return, which is outstanding!

I don't know of any other way of making a rate of return of 25% per year, every year, except by using the tax laws. Learn to use the tax laws. They can make you rich.

Finally, because Sandy contributed $2,000 of her earned income to her IRA, her taxable income was not $31,200 less her exemptions and deductions but only $29,200 less her exemptions and deductions. Therefore, she paid $400 (20% × $2,000) less in taxes than she would have if she hadn't saved and invested the $2,000 in an IRA.

The Roth IRA

In 1998, Congress voted for a new kind of long-term, tax-favored investment plan. It is the Roth IRA, named after Delaware Senator Joe Roth. Contributions to a Roth IRA are not tax-deductible like those to a regular IRA; however, the earnings are tax-exempt, unlike those of a regular IRA, where earnings are tax-deferred only until you withdraw them. You never pay tax on the earnings in your Roth IRA, not even when you take them out in retirement. This is the big benefit.

The earnings in a Roth IRA are not taxed as long as they are in the Roth at least five years and you are at least 59.5 years old when you withdraw them. Also, you are not required to take any money out of your Roth at age 70.5, as you are with a regular IRA. You can hold the money in your account until you die without any tax penalty.

Maximum contributions are $2,000 per year of your income if less than $95,000 (single taxpayer) or $150,000 (joint return). Both spouses may contribute to Roth IRAs.

One last point about a Roth. You can contribute to one even if you are participating in another qualified retirement plan.

The Education IRA

Also in 1998, Congress created the Education IRA. Contributions to an Education IRA are not deductible, but the earnings are tax-deferred, which is a big benefit. And the earnings are not taxed at withdrawal either, provided the money is used for higher education expenses. These expenses include tuition, books, and room and board. Any withdrawals not used for education expenses will be taxed and subject to a 10% tax penalty.

Anyone can set up an Education IRA for a child: a parent, grandparent, relative, or friend. The maximum contribution is $500 per year to each child. The contributions can be invested in bank CDs, government bonds, or mutual funds. Any money left in an account when the child turns 30 can be added tax-free to another child's Education IRA or else it must be distributed to the child within 30 days. That distribution is taxable and subject to a 10% tax penalty.

The two principles of tax-deductibility and tax-deferrability work in every qualified retirement plan. And everybody who is working for a living is eligible for at least one of these plans. If you are not taking advantage of these tax breaks for yourself, you are missing a great opportunity—and the easiest way to become rich. Whether you have an individual retirement account, a Keogh plan for the self-employed, a SEP-IRA, a SAR-SEP-IRA, a simple IRA, a 401(k) plan, or a 403(b) plan, the tax laws can be used to your advantage. Nobody likes to pay taxes. But whereas tax evasion is a crime, tax avoidance using the tax laws is not a crime; it is a choice you can make and the right choice that can, in fact, make you rich.

Home Mortgage Deductions

The second biggest single tax break available to you is the deductible interest on your home mortgage. Here again, the numbers are staggering. In chapter 1, I mentioned Charles and his wife, Cindy, who, at 40, owned their home and had two children ready for college. They bought their house for $200,000 with a 10% down payment of $20,000 and a mortgage of $180,000. In typical 30-year financing with a loan at a 10% interest rate, they will pay in interest to the bank or finance company approximately three times the amount of their mortgage. Three times $180,000 gives an approximate total cost of $540,000. Their actual cost will be $576,000. Subtract the $180,000 of loan principal, and they are paying approximately $396,000 in interest on their mortgage. Every penny of that $396,000 is a tax-deductible expense. The tax law gives homeowners a mighty tax break.

The payments on their $180,000 mortgage are $1,600 a month. Charles's best friend, Jerry, is renting a nice two-bedroom, two-bath apartment in the same neighborhood for $1,100 a month. That's $500 a month less than Charles's payment. Charles and his wife scrimped and saved to come up with the down payment because they always wanted to own their own home. Jerry, on the other hand, is glad to have the extra $500 a month in spending money and has no desire to be tied down by home ownership.

If you want to become rich, look at the big picture. Over the 30 years of their mortgage, Charles and his wife will pay $1,600 a month principal and interest. That's $19,200 a year, or $576,000 over 30 years. Jerry will pay $1,100 a month, $13,200 a year, for a total of $396,000 over the next 30 years, *if he doesn't get a rent increase.* Jerry gets no tax deductions for his $396,000 in housing costs. Charles and his wife are able to deduct all the interest they pay on their $180,000 loan, that is, $576,000 total payments less $180,000 principal, equaling $396,000 interest. They have $396,000 in tax deductions as part of their $576,000 in housing costs. The tax savings due to $396,000 of interest at a 20% tax rate is $79,200. Charles's and Cindy's housing cost for 30 years is their $200,000 purchase price plus $316,800 ($396,000 interest payments minus $79,200 tax savings) plus property taxes and insurance of approximately $70,000, for a total cost of $586,800. This is $190,800 more than Jerry will pay, and they own a $200,000 asset, not counting inflation. (Counting inflation at 4%, their house would be worth $648,000 after 30 years.) Jerry, on the other hand, owns nothing for the almost $400,000 he has spent in housing costs. Here again, using the tax laws will help to make you rich.

	Charles	**Jerry**
Payment per month	$1,600	$1,100
Payments per year	19,200	13,200
Payments over 30 years	576,000	396,000
Loan principal	80,000	0
Tax-deductible interest	396,000	0
($180,000 principal plus $396,000 interest = $576,000 total cost)		
Tax savings at 20% tax rate	79,200	0
(20% × $396,000)		
Actual cost after tax savings	495,800	396,000
($576,000 – $79,200 = $495,800)		
Value of property after 30 years with 4% inflation	648,000	0

Note: See chapter 5 to see the real cost to Jerry if inflation is 4% for the next 30 years.

If your house cost $100,000, cut these figures in half. If it cost $400,000, double these figures and double the amount of tax-deductible interest you will have. If your house cost $600,000, multiply the figures by 3; if $800,000, multiply them by 4.

Your Second Residence

The tax laws that allow you to deduct the interest you pay on your primary residence have been expanded to include a second residence as well. This could be a summer home at the shore, a winter condo in the mountains, a motorhome, or a yacht. It doesn't matter if your yacht is 20 or 120 feet long. If it has cooking, sleeping, and toilet facilities, it qualifies as a second residence and the mortgage interest can be deductible. You can even rent out your second home and still deduct the mortgage interest, as long as you use the home personally for at least 14 days a year or 10% of the number of days it is rented. You can rent it out 90% of the time and still deduct the interest.

The tax code is full of deductions. Use them to help make you rich.

Chapter 7
The Magic of Compound Interest: Time Is on Your Side

Over 200 years ago, Baron Rothschild said, "Compound interest is the eighth wonder of the world." He was right then and he still is. If you are going to be rich, you must know and understand the magic of compound interest—the magic of *earning interest on your interest.* Or as Ben Franklin said, "Your money can beget money and that money can beget more." Through the magic of compounding, what starts out as a tiny trickle of interest or dividends or capital gains can grow into a full torrent of money pouring into your accounts.

Ken Plans for Retirement

Here's a simple illustration. Ken, a computer programmer, decided to save $100 a month, which is $1,200 a year. He plans to invest this money in an income fund he found by researching *Morningstar Reports* at the library. The fund pays 9% a year, paid monthly. (We'll discuss why that is important later in this chapter.) Since the income fund is within his IRA plan, he won't have to pay any taxes on the savings. Ken is 28 years old, and he figured that if he saved just $100 a month at 9% interest, he could retire at 60—that is, in 32 years.

This is the way he figured:

Saving $1,200 a year for 32 years ($1,200 × 32) = $38,400

Then he added the interest like this:

Plus 9% interest on $1,200 the first year = $108
Plus 9% interest on $2,400 ($1,200 × 2) the second year = $216
Plus 9% interest on $3,600 ($1,200 × 3) the third year = $324
And so on until finally in year 32:
Plus 9% interest on $38,400 the last year = $3,456

Then he added all of this interest together, for all 32 years, and got a total of $54,648.

He then added this interest to his total principal, his total contributions over 32 years of $38,400, and he came up with $93,048. This is what he figured he would have to retire on. At 60, he could take out the interest of 9% on his IRA account of

$93,048 without any tax penalty. Nine percent of $93,048 = $8,374. He looked at that and knew it wasn't enough. He knew he couldn't get by on an income of just $8,374 a year, so he decided he would have to work to 65 and keep on building his retirement fund.

Using his method, at 65 he would have $44,400 in principal ($1,200 × 37 years) plus an additional 5 years of interest, as follows:

Plus 9% interest on $39,600 =	$3,564
Plus 9% interest on $40,800 =	3,672
Plus 9% interest on $42,000 =	3,780
Plus 9% interest on $43,200 =	3,888
Plus 9% interest on $44,400 =	3,996
	$18,900

Total interest earned to age 65: $18,900 + $54,646 = $73,548.

When Ken looked at these additional figures, he saw immediately that he was earning more in interest every year than the $1,200 he was contributing. In fact, he was earning three times as much in interest as his contribution! That's magic!

By working an extra five years to age 65, Ken figured he would then have $44,400 in principal plus $73,548 in interest, or a total of $117,948. This, at 9%, would give him $10,615 per year. This amount was a lot more than the $8,374 he had at age 60 but still not enough. Then he estimated his Social Security income at about $18,000 per year and added that to his $10,615. This would give him a total income of $28,615 a year, and he thought if he was careful he could get by on that.

Ken's Mistake

Of course, Ken made a *big mistake* in how he figured the value of his IRA. He ignored the magic of compound interest. He underestimated his wealth by *more than half!* He was using the calculation for simple interest, where the interest is paid out but not added to the account. In compound interest, each interest payment is added to the account and then this larger account earns interest. Here is what he actually will have, using the laws of compound interest. He invests $100 a month, $1,200 a year, for 32 years to age 60 in a mutual fund that is paying 9% interest a year, with dividends paid monthly. He also reinvests the dividends every month.

The first month he earns (9% ÷ 12 months) × $100 = .0075 × $100 = $0.75 or 75 cents.

The second month he earns .0075 × ($100 + $100 + $0.75) = .0075 × $200.75 = $1.51.

The third month he earns .0075 × ($200.75 + $100 + $1.51) = $2.27.

The fourth month he earns .0075 × ($302.26 + $100 + $2.27) = $3.03 and so on.

By using the correct formula for compound interest, Ken has earned $50.76 at the end of the first year, not the $108 he thought he would earn. This is because he only had $1,200 in his account for the last month, not for all 12. The other 11 months he had less money so he earned less. He starts his second year with $1,200 + $50.76, and earns interest on the total of $1,250.76. By his method, he earned interest on only $1,200.

The magic of compound interest, however, is in how it will build and build every year. At the end of the second year, he will actually have $2,400 + $218.85, not $216. (Refer to his figures on page 49.) After three years, he will have $3,600 + $515.27, not just the $324 he had figured. At the end of 32 years, when he is 60, he will have his contributions of $38,400 plus $183,251 in interest, for a total of $221,651 in his IRA, not the $93,048 that he had calculated. This is 3.3 times the interest earnings he had calculated. Now, if he earns 9% on this $221,651, he will have an income of $19,948, as opposed to the $8,374 he thought he would have.

Note that the money he will contribute over the years—$38,400—is only 17% of the total that will be in his IRA. He may struggle to save $100 per month every month for 32 years, yet his effort will generate only 17% of the money in his retirement account. The rate of return or interest earned, in conjunction with the time he will be invested, will make up 83% of his retirement account. This is true of all long-term investment accounts. And it will be true for yours.

The Magic Revealed

In this case, the magic of compound interest *more than doubled* Ken's investment results. He will have $221,651, not just $93,048. He will have 2.3 times more money than his simple system estimated.

The $19,948 he would earn in his IRA at age 60 was still not enough to live on, however, so he decided to work to 62, at which age he can collect 80% of his Social Security.

At age 62, he will have contributed $40,800 to his retirement plan and earned $227,005 in interest—5.3 times his contribution! That's magic, and you can use it, too.

Using the correct formula for compound interest, at age 62, Ken's IRA will have $40,800 plus $227,005 interest, for a total of $267,805. At 9%, this will pay him $24,102 a year, plus he estimates he will receive about $14,400 from Social Security. That will give him $38,502 a year. This is more than he thought he would have at age 65 ($28,600), and he thinks he can retire and live comfortably on that.

Note that his total contribution at age 62 of $40,800 is only 15% of his total account. This magic is the magic of compound interest over time. This is what will make you rich. Just think about this for a minute. If there was no interest at all, to have $267,000 at age 62, Ken would have to save $7,852 a year, or $654.33 a month every month for 34 years. That's about 25% of his salary. Luckily, with compound interest he can save less and still retire. His savings of $100 per month is only 3.82% of his salary. So he saves 3.82% of his income and lets the magic of compound interest do all the work. It provides 85% of his retirement income in this illustration. Note that this illustration ignores inflation. With inflation, Ken will need more than the $38,502 shown here to maintain his standard of living in retirement, but he will probably also get salary increases (due to inflation and increased job skills), so he can contribute more to his IRA over time.

Table 7.1   Interest Earned per Year on Savings of $100 per Month

Year	Save $100/mo	9% Simple Interest	9% Interest Compounded Monthly
1	$1,200	$108	$50
2	2,400	216	168
3	3,600	324	297
4	4,800	432	437
5	6,000	540	590
6	7,200	648	758
7	8,400	756	942
8	9,600	864	1,143
9	10,800	972	1,363
10	12,000	1,080	1,603
15	18,000	1,620	3,047
20	24,000	2,160	5,561
25	30,000	2,700	9,832
30	36,000	3,240	15,611
31	37,200	3,348	17,224
32	38,400	3,456	18,953
Totals after 32 years	**$38,400**	**$54,648**	**$183,251**
33	39,600	3,564	20,843
34	40,800	3,672	22,911
35	42,000	3,780	25,173
36	43,200	3,888	27,647
37	44,400	3,996	30,352
Totals after 37 years	**$44,400**	**$73,548**	**$310,177**
Total principal and interest		**$117,948**	**$354,577**

Points to Remember

Ken made two other mistakes that you should avoid when you think about your long-term investment results:

1. Ken thought he earned $108 in interest the first year; therefore, he thought he would earn $108 per year for each $1,200 he contributed. Instead, he will earn more every year because the interest compounds monthly. In reality, he earns interest on his interest, on his interest. His interest is compounded *384 times* (32 years × 12 months per year).

2. Ken will invest $1,200 a year for 32 years, which is $38,400; so at age 60 he figured he would earn 9% on $38,400. Instead, he will earn 9% on the total of all of his contributions to his IRA, which is $38,400 *plus* all the compound interest, the interest on his interest, figured every month, for a total of $183,251. His interest started at $50.76 the first year and will be $18,953 in the 32nd year. He will contribute $1,200 the last year and earn $18,953 interest! That is the beauty, and the magic, of compound interest.

This great amount of interest, $18,953 on a small $1,200 investment, is compelling. No one can afford to pass it up. Of course, you must start early to earn it. It is a gift of time. There is no get-rich-quick scheme that works. But over time, compound interest, or rate of return, works its magic.

Monthly versus Annual Interest

It makes a difference whether the interest is compounded monthly (the best), quarterly, or annually. If you have a $100,000 CD at 9%, the interest the first year would be $9,380 if it is compounding monthly versus $9,000 if it is compounding annually. Each year the difference becomes larger, so check to see *how your interest is compounded*.

Many banks and annuities pay interest only annually, especially on larger accounts. Yet some pay quarterly. Mutual funds and money market accounts generally compound their interest monthly. Take advantage of that. It's your money, and you have a choice. Know these principles, and make the right choice.

What is your bank paying now? If your bank is paying 5% for a one-year CD and another bank pays 6%, what is the difference? On $10,000 for one year, with annual compounding, the difference is $500 versus $600 = $100. For a $100,000 CD, the difference is $1,000.

The real question is, how long is your money going to be there? Ten years? Twenty years? Thirty years? Look at the difference time makes!

Table 7.2   Value of $10,000 CD at 5% Interest

	10 Years	20 Years	30 Years
Compounded annually	$16,289	$26,533	$43,219
Compounded monthly	16,470	27,126	44,677
Difference	$ 181	$ 593	$ 1,458

Table 7.3   Value of $100,000 CD at 5% Interest

	10 Years	20 Years	30 Years
Compounded annually	$162,890	$265,330	$432,190
Compounded monthly	164,700	271,260	446,770
Difference	$ 1,810	$ 5,930	$ 14,580

The difference in interest earned on $10,000, whether it is compounded monthly or annually, is not very large, even after 20 or 30 years. However, on $100,000 the difference is large and should be taken into account. Rich people know this and so should you.

As the interest rate, or rate of return, goes higher, the difference between monthly and annual compound interest gets larger.

Table 7.4   Value of $100,000 CD at 9% Interest

	10 Years	20 Years	30 Years
Compounded annually	$236,740	$560,140	$1,326,770
Compounded monthly	245,134	600,911	1,473,045
Difference	$ 8,394	$ 40,771	$ 146,275

This is a lot of money just for getting interest compounded monthly instead of annually.

Taxes and Inflation

Let's go back to Ken's IRA for another look. If Ken saved his IRA money in a simple bank savings account that paid 5% and inflation was 4%, he would gain only 1% a year. That's a very poor investment, yet many people do just that.

Ken made no allowances for taxes, which is correct because he used an IRA. He also made no allowance for inflation, which is not right. If inflation is 4% and he earns 9%, then his net increase is only 5%. If costs go up 4% a year, then he needs to earn 4% just to stay even. With 9% interest and 4% inflation, his net earnings are only 5% a year. For this reason, he should be looking at investments that pay more than 9% on average over the 30 to 35 years he will be building his retirement account.

Your Turn

The true magic of compound interest works every time. Money begets money. The rich get richer. Join them. Know the magic of compound interest and use it.

Take one more look at Form 1—Income and Form 2—Assets in chapter 2. Are all of your investments set up to use, and benefit by, compound interest?

Is your interest being reinvested? Are your dividends being reinvested?

Is your interest paid monthly? quarterly? or annually? Now you know the difference that makes, so move your money to accounts that *pay more* and *pay more often*. Let the magic work for you. It's your money and it's your choice.

Note: Some investments today earn as much as 9% but are not guaranteed, and no one knows what they will earn in 34 years, when Ken retires.

- AAA bonds and U.S. Treasury bonds currently pay 4.5–5.5%.
- High-yield bonds rated B and C pay about 6–9%.
- Some high-yield bond funds and international bond funds pay up to 8–9%.
- CMOs (collateralized mortgage obligations) pay 6–7%.

Good stock mutual funds have averaged over 12% and would probably be better for Ken over 34 years than a bond fund.

Part 3
The 10% Solution

Building your wealth can be accomplished using just 10% of your income. The key is to start early and make good choices.

The seven steps in the financial planning process are presented here, along with detailed examples showing their successful use.

Chapter 8
Following All Seven Steps

This chapter gives the complete solution to the question, "How can I become rich safely and easily and still lead a normal life?" Three complete plans are presented here for people 20–40 years old with earnings of $40,000, $70,000, or $120,000 per year. These plans show how to start, what to invest in, how much to invest, what insurance you need, and how much the insurance should cost. They also show the changes to make as the value of your accounts grows and they show the results: $2,000,000 or more.

The problem is how to become rich. The solution is

1. To know that it is possible if you give yourself some time.
2. To develop a simple plan.
3. To *start now!*

Start now by investing 10% of your income. Ten percent isn't very much. You could invest 15% or even 20%. (I know a man who always invested 50%. Half of everything he earned was invested; the rest he spent.) If you very specifically invest 10% of what you earn every year and follow the steps in this book, you will become rich in 30 to 40 years. Start in your 20s; retire in your 50s or 60s. With an average life span of 86 years you could be working and investing for less than half your lifetime.

Until you have tried it, the act of saving 10% of your earnings may seem impossibly difficult. If you look at your bills each month and then add on everything you need, or think you need, you will have no money left over for "savings." "Savings," you may rationalize, "is a nice idea, but I'm not going to retire for years and years, so I'll just have to wait a little while to begin saving."

You can say that for the rest of your life. Many people do. Look around you and you will see them everywhere. They far outnumber the wealthy few who carefully, consciously, and consistently build their wealth, who create their own riches.

What you have to do is make a commitment. Put 10% of your next paycheck into a new savings account. Then a week later, notice that you have survived for a whole week without your full paycheck. Then start thinking about how it's going to feel to be rich. Start planning it. You have just demonstrated that you can do it. Feel a little pride in your accomplishment. You've taken the first step.

You *can* invest 10% of your income and maintain your lifestyle. Once you get started, you won't notice the decrease in spending money at all. You have more than 10% withheld from your paycheck now for taxes, and you get along just fine. If your income is from commissions or is irregular, invest 10% of whatever you are paid. Sometimes it will be a lot, sometimes a little. The steady 10% is what counts.

Remember Sandy in chapter 1? She invested $2,000 in her IRA every year starting when she graduated from college. Her first year out of school, she earned $600 a week. Ten percent of that would have been $60: $60 × 52 weeks = $3,120 a year. She invested only $2,000 per year. After taxes and other deductions, her net pay was $428 a week. Ten percent of that is $42.80: $42.80 × 52 = $2.225.60 a year, which is still more than the $2,000 she actually invested. She invested less than 10% and she will have a comfortable retirement.

You can invest 10% of your gross income or 10% of your net income. The process will work either way. The key point is to save that 10% every payday. And the more you invest, the sooner you will get rich.

If your gross pay is $500 a week, you should plan to invest $50 a week. If you want to be conservative, you could figure 10% of your net pay, which is $500 less federal taxes of $60, less Social Security (FICA) of $31, less Medicare of $7.25, for a net pay of $401.75. You probably have state taxes and other items—perhaps insurance, union dues, or the like—deducted in addition to FICA and federal taxes. The point is to invest 10% of what you earn. That is more than enough to become rich, and you still will be able to cover all of your basic needs.

There is no point in getting rich at the expense of all that is valuable in life. Your family, your home, your community and friends, and your self-esteem are all important. Becoming rich does not mean you have to become mean or stingy. In fact, the more money you have, the more you can give of yourself. You will find that the more you give, the more you have to give. It's like the magic of compound interest: The more you have, the more you will receive. The more you receive, the more you can give. And it feels good when you give.

———

Let's look at a general outline of what three couples in the 20-to-40 age range should be doing with their money if they want to take care of their responsibilities, enjoy life fully, and get rich in the process.

We will look at three different income levels: $40,000, $70,000, and $120,000 per year. This income can come from one person or can be the combined income from two people. That doesn't matter. What is important is how the income is used.

In each case, exactly 10% of the income will be used to build wealth and take care of financial responsibilities. The rest is to spend any way the couples choose in their daily living and/or to pay taxes. The examples are intended to show you how to handle your money on a month-to-month basis, how to invest the 10% and spend 90%. All of these plans are laid out using the seven-step strategy described in chapter 3.

Annual Income $40,000

This is what a budget and financial plan for a couple in the 20-to-40 age group would look like if they earn $40,000 per year.

Table 8.1   Budget and Plan for Couple Earning $40,000

Income: $40,000 per year, $3,300 per month
Amount available to spend and pay taxes: $2,970 per month
Amount available to invest in wealth-building plan: $330 per month (10%)
The seven step financial planning process:

The Plan

1. Cash reserves:		Put $100 per month into your cash reserves until you have $6,000, which is about two months' expenses. Allocate the $6,000 like this:
		$1,000 Checking account cushion
		$2,000 Money market account at a bank or mutual fund
		$3,000 Tax-free bond fund with check-writing privilege
2. Insurance:	Auto:	$100,000/$300,000 liability; collision, uninsured motorist, fire, and theft coverage. Paid as part of normal car expenses; not paid as part of your 10% investment plan.
	Health:	$1,000 deductible. Paid at work if possible; otherwise, you pay for it. Not part of your 10% investment plan.
	Disability:	60% of salary for 2 years or more. If not available at work, take out an individual policy. Not an investment but very necessary.

Homeowners: Policy #5 (100% coverage of house at replacement value). Update value at least every 3 years. Not part of your investment plan.

Life: Necessary only when you have financial dependents. A $150,000 (minimum) universal life policy paid up at age 65 is preferable. If you absolutely cannot afford the universal   life, take out a 20-year term policy. Purchase life insurance at work, if available. Universal life insurance is part of your investment play because it has cash value; term insurance does not.

3. Guaranteed savings: When you have a minimum cash reserve of $3,000, start a tax-free bond fund as part of your cash reserves. It is also part of your guaranteed savings because of the higher interest it pays. Cash value is also building up in the life insurance policy after 2 years, another a form of savings.

4. Growth investments: First, invest all qualified retirement plan money in growth funds. Invest the maximum allowed by the retirement plan that fits within your 10%.

- IRA: $2,000/year; $166/month
- 403(b): Up to 16% of salary
- 401(k): Invest at least enough, usually about 6% of salary, to be eligible for the total company match. Then add as much more as you can afford.

Second, if you can invest more than your qualified plans allow, start a personal mutual fund account, a new Roth IRA account, or a variable annuity.

Note: When you have $6,000 in your cash reserve accounts, stop adding to them and add that $100 per month to your growth dollar accounts.

5. Tax planning: Use an IRA, or any other qualified retirement plan, for tax-deductible investments and tax-deferred growth. Cash value in the life insurance policy earns tax-free interest. A tax-free bond fund, new Roth IRA, and variable annuity all have big tax benefits. See chapters 6 and 16.

6. Retirement planning: Use an IRA or other qualified retirement plan, plus guaranteed savings, plus the cash value of your life insurance, plus cash reserves and Social Security income.

7. Estate planning: Use an IRA or other qualified retirement plan with a named beneficiary, plus your life insurance policy, plus a living trust.

This is a complete plan. If started early and followed without fail, this plan will lead to riches. Here, in simple form, is your money's cash flow into your wealth-building plan:

Cash reserves/savings:	$ 100 per month
Life insurance:	$ 64 per month
IRA:	$ 166 per month
Total:	$ 330 per month

This is 10% of your $3,300 monthly income and affordable for anyone with a $40,000-a-year income. If your income is somewhat more or less than this, adjust the figures up or down to suit your situation. And you can always add a little extra to your plan from time to time. You have choices.

Priorities

Start investing in this sequence:

Without children
1. Cash reserves/savings
2. Auto, health, disability income, and homeowner's insurance (if you own a home)

3. IRA
4. Other investments

With children   1. Cash reserves/savings
2. Auto, health, disability income, and homeowner's
    insurance (if you own a home)
3. Life insurance
4. IRA
5. Other investments

Annual Income $70,000

Using a similar process, this is what a budget and plan for a couple in the 20-to-40 age group would look like if they earn $70,000 per year.

Table 8.2   Budget and Plan for Couple Earning $70,000

Income: $70,000 per year, $5,800 per month
Amount available to spend and pay taxes: $5,220 per month
Amount available to invest in wealth-building plan: $580 per month (10%)
The seven-step financial planning process:

The Plan

1. Cash reserves: Put $225 a month into your cash reserves until
                               you have $4,000. Allocate $1,500 to a check-
                               ing account and $2,500 to a money market
                               account. Then start to put money into a tax-
                               free bond fund as backup to your cash
                               reserves. Keep building here until you have
                               $10,000 in these three accounts (checking,
                               money market, tax-free bond fund), which is
                               about two months' expenses. The $10,000
                               should break down like this:

$1,500	Checking account
$2,500	Money market account at a bank or mutual fund
$6,000	Tax-free bond fund with check-writing privilege

2. Insurance: Auto: $200,000/$500,000 liability; colli-
                               sion, uninsured motorist, fire, and

	theft coverage. Not part of investments.
Health:	$1,000 deductible. Paid at work if possible.
Disability:	60% of salary for at least 2 years. If not available at work, take out an individual policy. Not an investment but very necessary.
Homeowners:	Policy #5 (100% coverage of house at replacement value). Update at least every 3 years.
Life:	Necessary only when you have financial dependents. A $300,000 (minimum) universal life policy, paid up at age 65 is preferable. Purchase at work, if available.

3. Guaranteed savings: When you have a minimum cash reserve of $4,000, start a tax-free bond fund with check-writing privilege as backup cash reserves. When you have $10,000 in combined cash reserves and guaranteed savings, put the $225 per month into step 4 growth investments. Cash value is also built up in the life insurance policy after 2 years.

4. Growth investments: Invest $226 per month. First, invest all qualified retirement plan money in growth funds. Start an IRA or other tax-qualified retirement plan invested in growth mutual funds. For an IRA, invest $2,000 per year or $166 per month. If married, also open a spousal IRA and put $60 per month in it. That, added to your $166, brings your contribution up to $226 per month, or $2,712 per year. For a 401(k) or other plan, invest up to $226 per month in it. Or put this extra $60 per month into a growth mutual fund or Roth IRA. In addition, the $225 allocated to cash reserves is invested here in growth funds

or a variable annuity when your cash reserves
are at the proper level.

5. Tax planning: Use an IRA or other qualified plan. Cash value in
                          the life insurance policy earns tax-free interest.
                          A tax-free bond fund and variable annuity both
                          have tax benefits.

6. Retirement planning: Use an IRA or other qualified plan, plus a tax-free
                          bond fund, plus growth mutual funds and a
                          variable annuity, plus the cash value in the life
                          insurance policy.

7. Estate planning: Use an IRA or qualified plan with a named benefici-
                          ary, plus your life insurance policy, plus a living
                          trust.

This is a complete plan, which, if started early and followed without fail, will lead
to riches. Your cash flow would look like this:

Cash reserves/savings:	$ 225	per month
Life insurance:	$ 129	
IRA:	$ 166	if single ($226 total for two IRAs if married)
Investments:	$ 60	if single
Total:	$ 580	per month

This is 10% of your $5,800 monthly income and is easily affordable for anyone
with a $70,000-a-year income. You could probably do better than this.

Priorities

Start investing in this sequence:

Without children: 1. Cash reserves/savings
                          2. Auto, health, disability income, and homeowner's
                             insurance
                          3. IRA or other qualified plan
                          4. Other investments

With children: 1. Cash reserves/savings

2. Auto, health, disability income, and homeowners insurance
3. Life insurance
4. IRA or other qualified plan
5. Other investments

Annual Income $120,000

Using a similar process, this is what a budget and plan for a couple in the 20-to-40 age group would look like if they earn $120,000 per year.

Table 8.3   Budget and Plan for Couple Earning $120,000

Income: $120,000 per year, $10,000 per month
Amount available to spend and pay taxes: $9,000 per month
Amount available to invest in wealth-building plan: $1,000 per month (10%)
The seven-step financial planning process:

The Plan

1. Cash reserves:		Put $400 a month into your cash reserves, checking, and money market accounts, until you have $2,400. Then continue to add $200 per month to your cash reserves and start putting $200 per month into a tax-free bond fund as backup cash reserves. Keep building these accounts until you have $15,000 in them, which is about two months' expenses. The $15,000 should break down like this:
	$2,500	Checking account
	$2,500	Money market account at a bank or mutual fund
	$10,000	Tax-free bond fund with check-writing privilege
2. Insurance:	Auto:	$500,000/$1,000,000 liability; collision, uninsured motorist, fire, and theft coverage
	Health:	$1,000 deductible. Paid at work if possible; otherwise, you pay for it. Not part of your 10% investment plan.

Disability:	60% of salary for at least 2 years. If not available at work, take out an individual policy. Not an investment but very necessary.
Homeowners:	Policy #5 (100% coverage of house at replacement value). Update at least every 3 years.
Life:	Necessary only when you have financial dependents. A $600,000 (minimum) universal life policy paid up at age 65 is preferable. Purchase at work, if available.

3. Guaranteed savings: When you have a minimum cash reserve of $5,000, start a tax-free bond fund with check-writing privilege as backup cash reserves. When you have $15,000 in combined cash reserves and guaranteed savings, put the $400 per month into step 4 growth investments. Cash value is also built up in the life insurance policy after 2 years, which grows at a fixed rate of interest and is therefore part of your guaranteed savings.

4. Growth investments: Invest $350 per month. First, start an IRA or other tax-qualified retirement plan invested in growth mutual funds. With an IRA, invest $2,000 per year or $166 per month. If married, also open a spousal IRA and put $166 per month in it. That, added to your $166, brings your contribution up to $332 per month, or $4,000 per year, which is the maximum under the 1997 tax law. This leaves $18 to invest in a growth fund. For a 401(k) or other plan, invest up to $350 per month in it. Or put this extra $184 per month (after investing in one IRA) into a growth mutual fund or variable annuity. In addition, the $400 allocated to cash reserves is invested here in growth funds or a variable

annuity when your cash reserves are at the proper level.

5. Tax planning: Use an IRA or other qualified plan. Cash value in the life insurance policy earns tax-free interest. A tax-free bond fund and variable annuity both have tax benefits.

6. Retirement planning: Use an IRA or other qualified plan, plus a tax-free bond fund, plus growth mutual funds and a variable annuity, plus the cash value in the life insurance policy.

7. Estate Planning: Use an IRA or other qualified plan with a named beneficiary, your life insurance policy, and a living trust.

This is a complete plan, which, if started early and followed faithfully, will bring riches. Here, in simple form, is your monthly cash flow:

Cash reserves/savings:	$ 400 per month
Life insurance:	$ 250
IRA:	$ 166
Investments:	$ 184
Total:	$1,000 per month

This is 10% of your $10,000 monthly income and is easily affordable for anyone with a $120,000-a-year income. You could probably do better than this. You can always choose to add more and retire sooner.

Priorities

Starting investing in this sequence:

Without children
1. Cash reserves/savings
2. Auto, health, disability income, and homeowner's insurance
3. IRA or other qualified plan
4. Other investments

With children: 1. Cash reserves/savings
                         2. Auto, health, disability income, and homeowner's
                            insurance
                         3. Life insurance
                         4. IRA or other qualified plan
                         5. Other investments

Your Turn

These tables give you a good general idea of what your personal financial plan should look like if you are in the 20-to-40 age group and have made up your mind that you want to be rich—not just to "have some money someday" but to be rich, with $2,000,000 or more. The tables show you how to allocate the 10% of your income you must dedicate to this goal.

It's your choice.

Table 8.4 is a final list showing the dollar amounts of cash reserves recommended at each income level and the types of insurance coverage and investments recommended for financial security. Table 8.5 then shows the amount of income allocated to each step of the financial planning process.

Table 8.4   Basic Financial Plan, Ages 20–40

	Annual Income		
	$40,000	**$70,000**	**$120,000**
1. Cash reserves	$6,000	$10,000	$15,000
Checking	1,000	1,500	2,500
Money market	2,000	2,500	2,500
Tax-free bond	3,000	6,000	10,000
2. Insurance			
Auto	$100K/$300K	$300K/$500K	$500K/$1M
Health	$1K deductible 80/20	$1K deductible 80/20	$1K deductible 80/20
Homeowners	#5, replacement value	#5, replacement value	#5, replacement value
Disability	60% of salary, 2 years	60% of salary, 2 years	60% of salary, 2 years
Life	$150K universal	$300K universal	$600K universal
3. Guaranteed savings	Tax-free bond	Tax-free bond	Tax-free bond
4. Growth investments	$2,000 IRA or $2,250 Spousal IRA or 403(b), 401(k), or other qualified plan Mutual fund Variable annuity	$2,000 IRA or $2,250 Spousal IRA or 403(b), 401(k), or other qualified plan Mutual fund Variable annuity	$2,000 IRA or $2,250 Spousal IRA or 403(b), 401(k), or other qualified plan Mutual fund Variable annuity
5. Tax planning	IRA or other qualified plan Tax-free bond fund Cash value in life insurance Interest on home loan(s) Variable annuity	IRA or other qualified plan Tax-free bond fund Cash value in life insurance Interest on home loan(s) Variable annuity	IRA or other qualified plan Tax-free bond fund Cash value in life insurance Interest on home loan(s) Variable annuity

6.	Retirement planning	IRA or other qualified plan Tax-free bond fund Cash value in life insurance Mutual fund(s) Life insurance paid up Home mortgage paid up	IRA or other qualified plan Tax-free bond fund Cash value in life insurance Mutual fund(s) Life insurance paid up Home mortgage paid up	IRA or other qualified plan Tax-free bond fund Cash value in life insurance Mutual fund(s) Life insurance paid up Home mortgage paid up
7.	Estate planning	Named beneficiaries IRA or other qualified plan Life insurance Living trust	Named beneficiaries IRA or other qualified plan Life insurance Living trust	Named beneficiaries IRA or other qualified plan Life insurance Living trust

Table 8.5 Income Allocation to Financial Plan, Ages 20–40

	Annual Income		
	$40,000	**$70,000**	**$120,000**
10% monthly	$330	$580	$1,000
1. Cash reserves			
Add per month	$100	$225	$400
Total needed	6,000	10,000	15,000
2. Life insurance			
Monthly premium	$64	$129	$250
Minimum needed	150,000	300,000	600,000
3. Guaranteed savings dollars			
Tax-free bond fund	$100 after	$225 after	$176+$400
combined with	30 mos. to	18 mos. to	after 12 mos.
insurance cash value	60th month	43rd month	to 24th month
4. Growth investments			
IRA or other			
qualified plan	$166	$166 single	$166 single
		$187 w/spouse	$187 w/spouse
Personal fund acct.	$100 after	$60+$225	$184+$400+
	60th month	after 43rd	$176 after
		month	24th month
5. Tax planning	Requires no additional investments		
6. Retirement planning	Requires no additional investments		
7. Estate planning	Requires no additional investments		
Total	$330	$580	$1,000

Notes:
1. When cash reserves are at basic required levels, allocate that monthly addition to growth investments.
2. These are minimums. You can always allocate more.

Chapter 9
When Will I Be Rich?

You might be saying, "Ownership, inflation, compound rate of return over time—I'm using all of them and have a good plan, but where is all this leading? When will I be rich?"

To answer these questions, we need to look once again at the magical effects of compound interest, or compound rate of return, over time and apply what we've learned to the three situations (annual incomes of $40,000, $70,000, or $120,000) we examined in chapter 8.

Let's start with something specific—the tax-free bond fund. The interest rate earned will actually change over time, of course, just as interest rates change in the general economy. And the interest rate can—through compounding—drastically affect the amount of time it will take you to become rich.

Beginning at Age 25

Let's start with someone who is now 25.

The first example in chapter 8 shows how to invest 10% of a $40,000 annual income. Of this, $100 a month goes into cash reserves, which include a checking account, a money market fund, and the tax-free bond fund. Starting with nothing, you would have to invest for 30 months (2.5 years) to accumulate $3,000 in your checking and money market funds, as recommended. Then at age 27-1/2, you could begin saving $100 per month in a tax-free bond fund. Using the current average interest rate, the fund will earn 5.4% every year. If you continue this for 30 months, you will have $3,000 in the fund (plus $318.65 in interest). You will then be 30 years old. How much will this tax-free bond account be worth when you are ready to retire at 65 if you never add another dollar to it or withdraw from it?

If $3,318 is left to grow tax-free at 5.4% interest, compounded annually for 35 years, it will grow to $20,911. Compounded monthly, it will grow to $21,874. Remember that your cost in this is only $3,000, so your investment will multiply by seven—700%.

In the example using a $70,000 annual income, you put $225 per month into cash reserves until they total $4,000, which takes about 18 months. Then you put the

$225 into a tax-free bond fund for 27 months until it is worth $6,000. This gives a total cash reserve of $10,000. If you invest $225 at 5.4% for 27 months, you will have, with compound interest, $6,698, which is more than your minimum goal. Therefore, you can invest the $225 here for just 25 months, not 27, and you will have $6,191 in your account. You can add $225 to your growth accounts two months sooner, in this case after 43 months (18 + 25 = 43).

Left to grow at 5.4%, tax-free, with dividends reinvested monthly, this $6,191 will grow to $44,043 at age 65 (36 years and 5 months), also about a 700% increase.

In the example using a $120,000 income per year, with the same assumptions and techniques, the tax-free bond fund will be worth $10,113 after 35 months and grow to $74,576 at age 65. This sum grew from an investment of only $9,200—an increase of over 800%.

These are interesting numbers and show the power of compound interest, but they are a long way from the $2,000,000 we are looking for. To turn that $74,576 into $2,000,000 while earning only 5.4%, you would have to start at age 28 with an initial investment of $271,000, not the $10,113 actually available. Therefore, you must earn more than 5.4% on your investments if you plan to be rich.

As noted, since 1926, the U.S. stock market has grown at an average rate of 12% per year. This figure is basically a measure of the Standard & Poor's 500 stock index, with all dividends and capital gains reinvested. Using this average and applying it to our growth investments, let's look further at the three examples. (Note: As stated previously, this assumed rate of 12% is the average rate going back to 1926 and includes the Great Depression of the '30s. Since the start of the great bull market of the '80s and '90s in 1982, the S&P 500 has been averaging about 16% per year; and about 20% since 1990.)

A couple with an income of $40,000 per year puts $166 a month into an IRA, starting when one spouse is 25. If this IRA earns the average rate of return of the S&P 500, 12%, then when that spouse is 65, it will be worth approximately $1,711,000. If the couple increases their contribution by $100 a month starting at about age 30, after building up a cash reserve of $6,000 as recommended, and if the money is tax-sheltered (perhaps in a spousal IRA, Roth IRA, or variable annuity), they would have another $580,000 in that account at age 65. This, plus the $1,711,000 in the IRA, totals $2,291,000—way beyond the $2,000,000 goal.

In reality, however, these people, like most, would have to use some of their money from time to time—for a down payment on a house, emergencies, or college expenses, for example. But they could definitely lead a normal life, both happy and fulfilling, and accumulate $2,000,000, plus or minus a little, by the time they are ready to retire. It is possible, and it can be done by anyone who understands these principles and uses them well.

If you are earning $70,000 a year, it is easier. You have more to work with. You start out investing $226 per month ($166 IRA + $60 personal) in your growth funds right away at age 25 and continue to do this for 40 years. If all of this money is tax-sheltered, it will grow, averaging 12% a year, to $2,330,000 when you are 65. There it is, all in one place, and with one simple investment—over $2,000,000!

Of course, the family with an income of $120,000 per year can do even better. If these investors start at age 25 with $350 per month, assuming it is tax-sheltered and earning 12% to age 65, they will have $3,608,400, plus their other accounts. In fact, just using this account, they would reach $2,000,000 at age 60. (It would be $2,030,000, to be exact.)

So using the simple 10% solution, even early retirement is possible. Time is the big factor here. Time truly works wonders. Given sufficient time to invest, you will be rich.

All of these illustrations are for people beginning their plan at 25, which gives them 40 years to build their wealth. What about someone who doesn't begin until age 35 or 45 or 50?

Beginning at Age 35

Let's look at three possible scenarios for wealth building beginning at age 35.

Age 35, Earning $40,000 per Year

The family earning $40,000 per year was investing 10% of its income like this:

Cash reserves	$ 100	per month
Life insurance	64	per month (if needed)
IRA	166	per month
Total	$ 330	per month

If they had no major financial emergencies, then after five years—60 months—they would have the following amounts:

		Time Needed to Build
$1,000	checking account	10 months
2,000	money market	20 months
3,000	tax-free bond fund	30 months
318	interest	

Cash reserves	$6,318	60 months

IRA $166 × 12 = $1,992/yr @ 12%/yr for 5 yr = $14,173

Life insurance, approximate cash value: $2,000

After five years, at age 40, using this plan, they would have $6,318 (cash reserves) + $14,173 (IRA) + $2,000 (life insurance) = $22,491.

At this point, their cash reserves are adequate at $6,318. Of this, $3,000 is in checking and a money market fund and is needed for day-to-day expenses. These two accounts will go up and down every month. However, we will assume that the tax-free bond fund will not be needed for day-to-day expenses and therefore will keep growing at 5.4% per year. No new money will be added to it after it reaches $3,318 at the end of five years. The $100 a month that was being put into the bond fund can now go into a new growth investment fund, perhaps a spousal IRA. If so, then that investment is totally tax-deferred (using the tax laws); it's also a tax-deductible contribution for tax purposes (also using the tax laws).

From age 40 to 65, if this family has no major financial emergencies, this is how their wealth will grow.

	Cost/Year	**Growth Rate**	**Value at 65**
Tax-free bond fund	No cost	5.4%	$12,600
Life insurance (if needed)	$768	4–6% tax-free	40,000
IRA	$1,992 (tax-deductible and tax-deferred)	12%	538,400
Spousal IRA or other	$1,200	12%	179,200
Total at 65			$770,200

Two facts are very obvious here. First, this is *not* $2,000,000 and, secondly, waiting 10 years to start wealth building makes a huge difference. In fact, beginning at age 35 robs our couple of approximately $1,477,566. That's *robbery*, and these investors did it to themselves by waiting. That extra $1,477,566 is due primarily to the effect of compound interest. You must use compound interest and let time work for you.

In order to build wealth of $2,000,000 by age 65, starting at age 35, this family would have to invest $617 a month and earn 12%, tax-deferred. This is about 19% of their total income, and it would be very difficult—but not impossible—to do.

To accumulate $1,000,000 by age 65, anyone starting at age 35 would have to invest $308 per month at 12%. This is about 9% of a $40,000 gross income and could be done with a little extra effort. For example, start two IRAs immediately, delay the life insurance, and reduce the money flowing into cash reserves. Although this will generate $1,000,000, it is risky because you are not building any cash reserves and don't have the life insurance protection the head of a family needs. It would be better in this case to start investing as shown here for three years and then increase the monthly investment to $500, with the extra $150 going into growth funds. Invest 15% of gross income, rather than 10%, into your wealth building and have a balanced financial plan.

How many people do you know that have $1,000,000 in liquid investments at age 65? Very few. Most people don't make the decision to start building wealth soon enough. Not many people really start before they turn 40. At 40, people begin to look ahead and wonder if they can ever retire. At 40, it is *very* difficult to become rich using our $2,000,000 definition. You need to start early, long before age 40 for most people. This is why it is so important to educate your children so they will start early and carry on your attitude toward building and having wealth.

One last point here: If you start at 35 and build your wealth plan to age 75, you will have the same results as someone who started at 25 and built an account to 65, except for the cash value of the life insurance. It's the time you spend working your plan that is the key. You can compensate for a late start—you just have to choose to do so.

Age 35, Earning $70,000 per Year

Using the same parameters as above, these are the results using a $70,000 income. Starting at age 35, the family invests 10% of their income like this:

Cash reserves	$225 per month
Life insurance	129 per month (if needed)
IRA or 401(k)	166 per month
Other growth investments	60 per month
Total	$580 per month

After 18 months, the cash reserves—checking and money market—total just over $4,000, so they then put the $225 a month into a tax-free bond fund. In 25 more months, when they are 38.5, this bond fund will be worth $6,191. Then they let it grow by itself and add the $225 per month to their growth investments.

So, at age 38.5, this is what they'd have:

Cash reserves	$4,000; balance fluctuates; not part of plan
Tax-free bond fund	$6,191; no further additions; earns 5.4%
IRA and Roth or Spousal IRA	$12,414; $166 into IRA + $60 per month in separate account, both at 12%
Life insurance	$3,000

Now the $225 that built up their cash reserves is added to their investments, also at 12%, and all are allowed to grow to age 65. This is the result:

Tax-free bond fund	$25,700
IRA	538,400
Life insurance, approximate cash value	92,000
Other investments, tax-deferred	612,000
Total	$1,268,000

From age 38.5, when the cash reserve is built up to $4,000, to age 65, if they have no major financial emergencies, this is how the wealth will grow.

	Cost/Year	Growth Rate	Value at 65
Tax-free bond fund	No cost	5.4%	$25,700
Life insurance (if needed)	$1,548	4–6% tax-free	92,000
IRA	$1,992 (tax-deductible and tax-deferred)	12%	538,400
Spousal IRA or other ($60 + $225 = $285/mo)	$3,420	12%	612,000
Total at 65			1,268,000

This is over $1,000,000, if all goes smoothly, but a lot less than $2,000,000. If they continued the process to age 67.5—only 30 more months—they would go over the $2,000,000 mark.

Age 35, Earning $120,000 per Year

Finally, the family earning $120,000 per year, following this same procedure, starting at age 35, will have this much in various investments at age 65:

Tax-free bond fund	$75,400
IRA or 401(k)	538,400
Life insurance	191,000
Other investments at	
$184/month × 12	596,600
Plus $400/month excess	
from cash reserves	1,026,800
Total	$2,428,200

The family makes its $2,000,000 goal easily using the simple 10% plan.

Beginning at Age 45

It should be clear that if you wait to age 45 to begin building your wealth, you won't make it. At least you won't have $2,000,000 in liquid investments at age 65 using the simple 10% plan, even if you earn $120,000 per year.

Age 45, Earning $40,000 per Year

Starting at age 45, using these same simple investment procedures until age 65, the couple earning $40,000 per year would then have the following:

Tax-free bond fund	$7,300
IRA	160,700
Life insurance	10,000
Other investments	50,100
Total	$228,100

Starting at age 45, using these same simple investment procedures until age 65, the couple earning $70,000 per year would then have the following:

Tax-free bond fund	$14,800
IRA	160,700
Life insurance	21,000
Other investments	197,800
Total	$394,300

Starting at age 45, using these same simple investment procedures until age 65, the couple earning $120,000 per year would then have the following:

Tax-free bond fund	$25,700
IRA	160,700
Life insurance	42,000
Other investments	609,600
Total	$838,000

Don't let these numbers scare you or upset you. They are based on very specific circumstances. Everyone's circumstances are different, and your numbers will be unique. *The idea here is to demonstrate to you that anyone—at any income level— can become richer than he or she is today.* Learn the principles and start. You have choices every day. The question is whether to start now or wait until next year or next month or until the car is paid off. The right answer is to start *now*—today, before you go to bed tonight.

You also have a choice of whether you should invest $100 or $75 or maybe just $50 to start with, until you get used to it. Don't get used to it. Do something new; get *rich*. You're used to not being rich. Start by investing $125 and get used to that! You deserve to be rich. You can afford it. You probably don't need all the things you buy!

Not only do you have a choice about *when* you will decide and begin and how much you will begin with, but also you have a choice of *where* you will invest your money. This decision requires your full attention. You know you will never get rich putting your money in a bank, where it is guaranteed up to $100,000 but earns very little in interest and therefore does not grow. And you'll never get rich putting your money in U.S. Treasury bonds, which are even safer than banks. Both of these investments are taxable loans. You need tax deferral, so you get to keep all—100%—of your earnings, and you need ownership. You need 12% or more. That's how you get rich.

You will probably need help in your pursuit of riches, and help is available. You'll find good professional advisors everywhere. But be careful: you'll also find bad professional advisors everywhere. You need to research, ask questions, check an advisor's record with regulatory agencies, and get referrals before you decide which advisor to use. Then, when you have chosen your advisor, check your results every quarter and every year. If you don't like what you see, change advisors.

You can become rich, but you need to get involved in the process. Be aware. You may need to make changes as you go along. You may need to change brokers, change advisors, change strategies, change investments. But don't change your mind. Decide to leave the realm of "I wish I were," "Someday I'm going to," or "If I ever had a chance." You do have a chance. The choice is up to you.

Chapter 10
If You're Over 50

As we've just seen, the longer you wait to start becoming rich, the smaller the result. It's as simple as that. But if you are over 50, don't be discouraged. Many, many people who take control of their finances in their 50s have a safe and comfortable retirement. Some even reach real wealth.

The key is, don't give up! There are many steps you can take that will move you closer to your goals: financial success and real wealth.

Many people, when they turn 50 or so, suddenly realize that they will want to retire someday—soon. They realize they have no plan for retirement; they have little or no money in retirement funds; their jobs don't offer pensions; they know nothing about investing or financial planning. Suddenly, they are faced with a big dose of reality—retirement—and they don't have any idea as to what to do about it. They're scared. They feel alone. In fact, some of their friends seem to have retirement plans working for them already. Some are talking about retiring *early*. They don't think they can ever retire.

Your Attitude

The first step if you are in this position is to affirm your attitude. You (and your spouse if you are married) must say, "I am going to retire. I am going to work at it, and nothing is going to stop me. After good health, good family, and good friends, a comfortable retirement is my number one priority." Remember, money isn't everything, but it is essential and useful.

Your Goal

Once you've firmed up your new attitude, affirm your goal. For example, "I am going to retire at 65." Having a goal is step two.

Your Inventory

Your next step is taking inventory. What do you have? What do you need? What is your income? How can you improve it? Go through Form 1—Income and then Form 2—Assets from chapter 2 again, being extra careful and thorough. People are often surprised to see how much they already have, how much money they have to work with. You may have more than you thought. Equally important as knowing your income is knowing and using your assets. Study them. First look at the noninvestment assets. What can you sell or give to charity? What needs fixing so it can be used? What is just surplus or junk? With your new attitude, be honest and decisive.

Income and Investments

Perhaps you can generate extra income. Maybe you can work overtime or on weekends. Now that the children are grown, perhaps your spouse can go back to work. Perhaps you can rent out a room of your house.

Do *everything* you can to build your income. And remember that spending less is almost the same as earning more. If your children are grown and out of the house (or almost out), you can probably spend less on them. Spending less on them means you can put more into your retirement and wealth-building plans.

With your new attitude, you can make new choices. The possibilities are endless. You can choose to use your money differently. You can put more of it, a *lot* more of it, into your retirement, your wealth. You can choose to spend less. Buy fewer new clothes, drive cars longer, eat out less often, spend less on vacations. In your 20s and 30s, you had to buy furniture, cars, televisions, clothes. Now you have all that and you don't *have* to buy them again.

Then look at your investment assets. Most people are surprised, when they list *everything*, at how much they really have. Probably you'll find no big accounts, but the little ones add up—extra checking accounts, a couple of small savings accounts, two or three little IRAs from years ago, and more. Maybe you have some old U.S. savings bonds, cash value in a small (or large) life insurance policy, or a few shares of stock.

Maybe you have none of these items, but maybe you do. If you do, combine, consolidate, and then put what you have into the best investments available. Don't hesitate. It's for you, your retirement, and your wealth. You will probably need a good financial planner to help you do this. (See chapter 15 for advice on how to choose one who is right for you.)

Consolidate Your Assets

Here are some ideas on how to consolidate assets.

- Combine all of your IRAs into one account, all of your spouse's into another. Then choose one or two good growth funds and invest each of your new consolidated IRAs into them. Manage these IRAs to give you the growth you need,

Remember, IRAs are tax-deferred, and growth funds are the best places to earn big capital gains. Even if you can no longer add to your old IRA because you now are covered by a retirement plan at work, such as a 401(k) plan, make the old IRA a good investment and keep track of it from now on. It will add to your wealth.

- Combine your checking accounts. Most families need only one, two at the most. Choose an account at a bank or credit union that is conveniently close and that costs little or nothing. Excess cash here should be invested in tax-free bond funds, up to a few thousand dollars, and the rest put into good growth funds.
- Close out small savings accounts and invest the money in a single money market account at a local bank, or better yet at a mutual fund that is paying the best rate of interest available: 4% to 5.5%, perhaps 2% or 3% more than you were getting. When you have a few thousand dollars in your money market account, then put the excess in tax-free bond funds or growth funds or into a safe, tax-deferred variable annuity.
- Combine small amounts currently in a variety of mutual funds into one good growth fund, watch it carefully and add to it often.
- Do the same with stocks. If you own some shares that you have held for years, it may be best to sell them, pay the taxes now, and invest the proceeds into your growth accounts.
- Cash in old U.S. savings bonds and replace them with current tax-free bond funds or growth funds.

Increase Your Investing

Adding to your investments is more important than ever when you are over 50. Your new attitude must be to build wealth, and you must build it fast. You don't have the time that a 20-year-old or 30-year-old or 40-year-old does. Instead of a 10% solution, you probably need a 20% solution, maybe even a 25% solution. (See chapter 8.)

If you have a retirement plan at work, such as a 401(k), contribute the maximum to it. Every dollar contributed is tax-deductible; therefore, your contribution reduces your taxes and builds your wealth. If you don't have a plan available at work, start an IRA. Under the 1997 tax law, both spouses can put up to $2,000 a year into an IRA, even if only one is working. Then look at a Roth IRA and a tax-deferred variable annuity for additional investing opportunities. If you have your own business on the side or are earning extra income from another job or business, set up a second retirement plan for yourself based on the income from that second business. Tax-qualified retirement plans are the most efficient investments available, because of the tax benefits.

If you have your own business, you can have an IRA or a Keogh plan, a profit-sharing plan, a money purchase pension plan, a SEP-IRA, a SIMPLE IRA, or a SAR-SEP-IRA. There are many choices. Some allow you to put away up to 25% of your income or $35,000, whichever is less, tax-deductible and tax-deferred. (Talk to your financial planner and tax accountant.)

If you are over 50 and want to be rich and retire in comfort, or at least feel rich, and you don't see how you possibly can, you must sit down and study your present situation honestly and in detail. Then make new choices. You will have to change your behavior if you want to change your future—to build wealth where there was none before.

Debt

Before we discuss the building of income and assets of a 50-year-old who is just beginning to plan seriously for his or her retirement, we have to think a little about debt. It is so easy to fall into debt these days. Easy credit terms and credit cards are available to almost everyone. And, of course, you can't build wealth and become rich if you have a mountain of debt. The two don't mix very well. Debt payments too often use up all the money that should be going into retirement and wealth-building plans.

Borrowing and time payment plans, such as a home mortgage or an auto loan, work well if the payments fit within your budget. But when your monthly payments are so great that there isn't 10% remaining in your budget for your wealth-building plan, then you are too deeply in debt. Your house mortgage generally shouldn't exceed 35% of your income; 25% is a much better figure. Mortgages and car loans together should not be more than 40% of your income.

For many people, debt is a big obstacle to wealth. With your new attitude, you must face your debts and the old habits that allowed the debt to build. You have to make new choices, which must include the following:

1. No new debt, no exceptions. There is always an alternative to acquiring more debt, including doing without.
2. A plan to pay off the old debt. Look at the plan from several angles, such as these:
   a. Make maximum payments every month. The idea is to pay off your debt as quickly as possible. If you are paying $800 a month on your debts now, could you pay $1,000? If you're paying $1,500, could you pay $2,000? Getting rid of the debt frees up income to invest in your retirement plan. If it is still going to take you two or three or four years, even with maxi-

mum payments, to pay off your debts, that means you are delaying the start of your retirement plan by two or three or four years, and that is not acceptable, especially if you're over 50.

b. Make minimum payments. Pay the minimum asked for on each account each month. This stretches out the time required to pay off the debt, but it may *free up current income* to invest into your retirement plan. You must start investing as quickly as possible to get the magic of compound interest working for you. That does more to build wealth than any other strategy.

c. Use a combination of a and b. This works for most people. Pay off the highest interest rate loans and credit cards first as quickly as possible, and stretch out the others so you can put as much money as possible into your retirement plans.

d. Take out a debt-consolidation loan. Sometimes a new loan taken out just to pay off all your old debts is the right solution. A new fixed and moderate interest rate loan may reduce your total cost of repayment substantially. And if the new loan payments are less per month than the combined payments on all the old bills, then you will have accomplished something useful. You will have more money each month to invest in your wealth-building plan.

Home Equity Loan

If you qualify, a home equity loan works especially well. These loans usually charge 8% to 12%, which is much less than many credit cards charge. Also, the loan interest is a deductible expense on your tax return because it is interest on your home loan, whereas the interest on your credit cards, auto loans, and other bills is not deductible. Thus, a home equity loan can cut your taxes substantially, while it improves your debt picture.

Always keep in mind, however, that you can't just pay off debt. You must build wealth. Sometimes, it is necessary to use your money only for debts for a few months, or for even a year, to pay your way out of a sudden, expensive emergency or crushing debt load. But once you have your debt under control, you can reduce—but not stop—your debt payments and start your wealth-building program. Pay off the old and begin the new. As you see the new begin to grow, you will be more and more eager to get rid of the old. There is great satisfaction, a sense of accomplishment, in making that last payment, whether it is on a car, your home, or a credit card.

Your Needs Come First

One final point here for 50-year-olds: You must take care of *your* financial needs ahead of everyone else in the family. If you are not financially strong, you can't possibly help anyone else to become strong.

Be firm with your children and firm with yourself. Don't spend your money on them now. If you do, you won't have it later and neither will they. Invest it now and you will all be much better off later. If your parents need financial help, be generous, but remember your own needs, too. Being firm can get difficult at times. You must be strong to be able to help others. Do what is right for all concerned.

How to Start—A True Story

John and Cathy are a typical example of a couple in their 50s, who realized they were unprepared for retirement. He was 54; she was 52. He worked in accounting for a small manufacturing company. Together, they filled out Form 1—Income and Form 2—Assets, which looked like this:

Form 1   Income

His job	$46,000
Savings interest (3 accounts)	81
Bond interest (14 U.S. savings bonds)	24
Life insurance (approximately 4 policies)	220
Mutual fund dividends (2 funds)	756
Stock dividends (2 stocks)	191
401(k) earnings (new last year)	188
IRAs (3)	329
	$47,789

(Note: The earnings in his 401(k) plan and IRAs are not taxable but definitely are part of his wealth-building plan, so they must be included here.)

Form 2   Assets

FINANCIAL ASSETS

Checking Accounts	
His, bank A	$546
Hers, bank B	788
Joint, credit union	1,121
Total checking accounts	$2,455
Fixed-Rate Savings Accounts	
Bank A, opened 2 years ago when John took out	
a car loan	$1,078
Bank B, opened 3 years ago when they were	
going to remodel	531
Credit union	2,463
Bank in Connecticut, never transferred	
when they moved to California in 1980	1,423
Total bank savings	$5,495
Life Insurance cash value	
His: $5,000 policy (bought for John by his father	
when he was 6 years old)	$2,114
$5,000 policy (bought when they were married)	1,891
$1,000 policy (bought in John's senior year at college)	546
Hers: $2,000 policy (bought when they were married)	746
U.S. Treasury bonds: 12 @ $25.00 and 2 @ $50.00	400
IRAs (3) in bank savings accounts	8,063
Total other fixed-rate savings	$13,760
Total all checking, savings, and other fixed-rate accounts	$21,710

Investment Accounts

Mutual fund A, growth	$1,788
Mutual fund B, growth and income	3,560
401(k) retirement plan	4,600
Delta Airlines stock, 200 shares (inherited in 1984)	8,957
Texaco stock, 80 shares	3,861
Total investments	$22,766
Total financial assets	$44,476

NONFINANCIAL ASSETS

Home, refinanced in '93, 7-$\frac{1}{2}$%, 30-year mortgage, took out an additional $40,000 to remodel and pay bills, currently owe $170,000 ($250,000–$170,000 = $80,000 net equity)	$250,000
'98 Buick Riviera (his), owe $9,000 ($14,000–$9,000 loan = $5,000 equity)	14,000
'91 Toyota Corolla (hers), paid for	2,000
'74 Chevy Nova (his), always liked it; still runs well and looks good; needs a little work but is paid for	1,000
Furniture and household goods	20,000
2 shotguns, rifle, and pistol; he has not been hunting since they left Connecticut	2,500
Haviland china, her mother's; she never uses it	2,000
Total nonfinancial assets	$291,500
TOTAL ALL ASSETS	$335,976

Total all assets	$335,976
Less home mortgage	–170,000
Less car loan	–9,000
Net value all assets	$156,976

Of course, your income and your assets will look completely different from these. But the principals and strategies are the same.

John and Cathy's Plan—Income

This is how John and Cathy proceeded.

1. All the interest earned and dividends received on investments are *extra* income; they are not to be used for living expenses but added to the wealth-building plan. These funds must be invested or reinvested. For example, John and Cathy will take the $81 of interest earned in their three savings accounts and invest it in *one* of the mutual funds and do this every year.

2. Ten percent of John's $46,000 salary is $4,600; 20% is $9,200. How much of this earned income—how much of your income—can and should be invested each year? In this example, John's employer offered a new 401(k) plan. If the plan will let John contribute 10% or more of his salary, and many do (some up to 15%), he can invest $4,600 or more there. This contribution is deductible from income each year for tax purposes, and all growth and earnings are tax-deferred. The other $4,600, if he decides he can afford it, could go into a good variable annuity. The money invested in a variable annuity is not tax-deductible, but all growth and earnings are tax-deferred, so it grows much faster than a similar mutual fund that is not tax-deferred.

3. Cathy decided to take a part-time job as secretary of their church as a way to increase the couple's income and, at the same time, do something useful for an organization to which she wanted to contribute. It only paid $80 a week, but she could put all of the money into their retirement plans. In fact, $2,000 of the $4,000 she would earn (50 weeks × $80 = $4,000) could go into an IRA. The remaining $2,000 is to be invested in the variable annuity.

John and Cathy's Plan—Assets

Looking at their list of assets, John and Cathy saw two concerns right away.

1. They didn't have nearly enough money invested—assets—to even think about retiring. They couldn't come close to meeting their retirement needs and keep pace with inflation with the assets they had. Therefore, they agreed to invest 10% of their current income right away and as much more as possible. They also agreed to invest all of their extra income, including the income from Cathy's new part-time job.

2. It seemed to them that they had a lot of little savings accounts and investments but no real plan for, or focus, to their financial assets. Therefore, they started asking their friends if anyone could recommend a good financial advisor to help them. After interviewing several certified financial planners who had been recommended and attending two seminars, they selected a woman of their own age, with over 15 years' experience in investing and insurance and a strong financial planning background, to be their advisor.

She agreed that they had too many small savings and investment accounts and, after two meetings with John and Cathy and careful consideration and analysis on her part, she recommended that they rearrange their assets like this:

Form 1   Income (Revised)

	Old	New
His job	$46,000	$46,000
Her job (new)	0	4,000
Savings interest (was 4 accounts totaling $5,495, now 1 for $3,000 at 5%)	81	150
Bond interest (was 14 bonds, now 0)	24	0
Tax-free bond fund (new; $2,495 from savings and $400 from their 14 U.S. savings bonds; earns 4.5%)	0	135
Life insurance (was 4 policies, 3 on John for $11,000 and 1 on Cathy for $2,000; now 1 on John for $100,000)	220	318
Variable annuity (new)	0	921
Mutual fund dividends (sold, added to variable annuity)	756	0
Stock dividends (stocks sold, added to variable annuity)	191	0
401(k) earnings (new last year, tax-deferred)	188	188
IRAs (was 3, now 1 apiece)	329	82
Total income	$47,789	$51,794

They followed their financial advisor's advice and made major changes in all areas, always moving toward higher earnings, lower taxes, and better growth prospects. They used inflation and knew that over time they would achieve significant results.

Their annual income went up by $4,005, of which $4,000 was from Cathy's new job. Most of the small items of income went up except for their stocks and bonds, which they sold, and the IRAs. Their IRA income went down because they transferred their IRAs from bank savings accounts, where they earned about 4% in interest, to growth mutual funds, where their dividends were less than 1%. However, their increase in *share price*—which is not income—*averaged over 12% per year.*

They made even more changes. John and Cathy closed three of their four savings accounts, keeping only their credit union account, which paid the highest interest at 5%. They put $3,000 in it, about one month's expenses, and put the remainder into their new tax-free bond fund, which pays 4.5%, totally tax-free. They sold their U.S. Treasury bonds and added the proceeds to their tax-free bond fund. The bond fund gave them flexibility and immediate access to their money, two benefits that they did not have with the treasury bonds.

They transferred the two IRAs from John's bank to a new growth fund IRA and did the same with Cathy's IRA. Because of her new job, she now planned to add to her IRA every year.

John and Cathy also cashed in their four small life insurance policies and rolled over the cash value into a new $100,000 universal life policy on John. The idea was that if he should die before they retire, Cathy would have another $100,000 to invest for her retirement income. The $5,297 cash value would continue to grow tax-free, and a large part of each premium paid on the policy went into the cash value, too. If he lives, and the odds are about 20 to 1 that he will, the cash value in the policy will grow to about $20,000, tax-free, that can be part of their retirement program.

As for their investments, John and Cathy sold their two mutual funds and invested the proceeds in the aggressive growth portfolio of a variable annuity. They also sold their two stocks and added that money to their variable annuity. These four items were now all growing, tax-deferred, in a professionally managed portfolio, as opposed to their previously amateurish and uninformed efforts.

John and Cathy each had a new IRA in a growth mutual fund, and John's 401(k) plan was also invested in a growth portfolio. They now expect that in 11 years, when he is 65, they will be able to retire in comfort.

John is contributing $4,600 a year to his company's 401(k) plan and getting a nice tax deduction for doing it. His employer is also contributing matching funds to the plan. In his case, the company contributes 50 cents for each $1.00 John contributes up to 6% of his salary. Six percent of $46,000 is $2,760. The company matches 50%, so it puts in $1,380 each year. This is a tax-free gift for John. The company does not match any of the additional 4% John contributes each year to his account. Cathy is contributing $2,000 a year to her new IRA for additional tax savings and another $1,700 to their variable annuity. (They will have to pay about $300 income tax, 15%, on Cathy's $4,000 income.)

John and Cathy plan to let the interest accumulate in their credit union account because they will use that account from time to time. They will also let the interest accumulate in the tax-free bond fund and John's new life insurance policy.

All the earnings inside the 401(k), IRAs, and variable annuity compound are tax-deferred, which is a big benefit for them.

Form 2   Assets (Revised)

	Old	New
Checking accounts		
His, bank A (now a joint account)	$546	$1,000
Hers, bank B (closed)	788	0
Joint, credit union (used mostly by Cathy)	1,121	1,000
$455 saved; added to their tax-free bond fund		
Total checking accounts	$2,455	$2,000
Fixed-rate savings accounts		
Bank A (closed)	$1,078	$0
Bank B (closed)	531	0
Credit union (one month's expenses)	2,463	3,000
Bank in Connecticut (closed)	1,423	0
Life insurance cash value (had 4, now 1)	5,297	5,297
U.S. Treasury bonds (sold)	400	0
Tax-free bond fund (new)	0	2,895
IRAs (3) at banks	8,063	0
Total fixed-rate savings	$19,255	$11,192

Investment accounts

Mutual fund A, aggressive growth	$1,788	$0
Mutual fund B, aggressive growth	3,560	0
401(k)		
John's contribution	4,600	4,600
Company match	1,380	1,380
Delta Airlines stock (200 shares)	8,957	0
Texaco stock (80 shares)	3,861	0
Variable annuity, tax-deferred		
(new from 2 mutual funds plus proceeds		
from selling Texaco and Delta stock)	0	18,166
IRAs (2 new)	0	8,063
Total investments	**$24,146**	**$32,209**
Total financial assets	**$43,401**	**$43,401**

John and Cathy have accomplished three goals by completely reorganizing their finances and investments:

1. They have decreased the number of their accounts.
2. Each account now has a specific purpose, and all the accounts together are focused on achieving their goal of retiring when John is 65. They have a financial planner helping them and top mutual fund managers managing their investments.
3. They are adding 10% of John's income to their investments, plus the $1,380 company match, plus 85% of Cathy's new income, plus an additional $1,200 per year, plus the tax-free compounding of all earnings in their 401(k), their two IRAs, their variable annuity, and John's life insurance policy.

And they are not quite finished. They know that investing 10% is enough for a couple in their 20s, but they need to invest a lot more than that when in their 50s, so they plan to also add $100 a month from John's income to their retirement plan. This is the additional $1,200 mentioned above. This will not be easy, as it involves certain changes in their lifestyle and habits, but they have a clear goal and they are determined to reach it.

Altogether, then, their annual investments in their new plan look like this:

John's 401(k) contribution	$4,600
Company match	1,380
Cathy's new IRA	2,000
Remainder of Cathy's salary, less tax	1,700
Joint investment of $100 per month	1,200
	$10,880 per year

For the next 11 years, they plan to invest $10,880 per year into their new retirement plan. That's $119,680. If their new growth funds average 12% per year, this will grow to about $276,800! The $10,880 a year they are investing is 21% of their total income, but they have extra income (Cathy's), some of their investments will reduce their taxes, and they have a goal and a plan and they are determined.

In addition, they now have $18,166 in their variable annuity. If it averages 12% growth, that could become another $63,000, and the $1,200 a year they are adding to it could grow to another $27,000. Plus they have their two IRAs worth $8,063, their tax-free bond fund, and the cash value inside their insurance policy.

Here's a comparison of the value of their investments now and at age 65:

	Current Value	Value at Age 65
Life insurance cash value	$5,297	$10,500
Tax-free bond fund	2,895	4,950
401(k)		
John's contribution	4,600	
Company match	1,380	
Total 401(k)	5,980	152,300
John's IRA rollover	8,063	28,000
Cathy's IRA	2,000	46,600
Variable annuity	18,166	120,200
	$42,401	**$362,550**

If they stick to their plan, they could have over $350,000 in their retirement plan when John is 65. That's not $2,000,000, but it is enough to retire on with Social Security.

Using these figures, their income in 11 years might look like this:

$400,000 at 6% (safe government bonds)	$24,000
John's Social Security at $1,200/month	14,400
Cathy's Social Security at $500/month	6,000
Total	$44,400

That's almost as much as John is earning now! And he will actually have more spendable income because he doesn't have to put $10,800 a year into his retirement plan. These estimates show that it can be done. Even with a late start, John and Cathy will achieve their goal.

The Extra Effort

Finally, John and Cathy took a hard look at all they had and made the decision that they really didn't want to be poor or worry about money for the rest of their lives. They were willing to put everything they had into their wealth-building and retirement program. They didn't want to take any chances or come up short.

Therefore, John is planning to sell his two shotguns and the rifle. One shotgun is an Ithaca, featherweight, 20-gauge that he bought for Cathy and that she fired only once. He carried it a few times, but it couldn't compare to his Remington 12-gauge automatic shotgun, which he doesn't use any longer. He doesn't need his 30.06 Winchester rifle, either. On the other hand, he has always enjoyed his Smith and Wesson pistol and just likes having it around the house.

Cathy is checking prices on the Haviland china and now thinks it may be worth closer to $6,000 than the $2,000 she originally thought. She felt a little guilty at first about even thinking of selling her mother's china, but her mom has been dead for six years now, and Cathy knows the china is hers to use as is best for her. She has decided to keep the teapot, sugar and creamer, and four cups and saucers, and she will start to use them. She will sell the 12 place settings and all the other pieces.

John is also cleaning up his Chevy Nova and thinks he might get $1,500 or $2,000 for it now. He has decided that he'd rather have the money in his retirement plan and live well for another 30 years than have that '74 Chevy in the garage (and Cathy's Toyota parked outside all the time).

The proceeds from the sale of these items comes to about another $10,000 that they will have to invest now. It could grow to almost $30,000 by the time they retire. And they are not really losing the things they are selling. John still has all the memories of each of his hunting trips and all the excitement—and struggle—they entailed. Cathy has a beautiful antique tea set and fond memories of how her mother spread the whole gorgeous china set on her dining room table when the family was together for holiday dinners. And John has pictures to look at and stories to tell about his '74 Chevy Nova.

Those memories never die. And their new investments will help them live in comfort while they enjoy those memories in their retirement and old age.

This is how John and Cathy, 54 and 52, began their wealth building plan. A plan like this will also work for you.

Chapter 11
Opportunities Unfold All around You

Wherever you are in life, this seven-step process will work. At your present age and your present income, fit yourself into the framework we have established here and get started.

Put 10% of your income into *your* get-rich plan. If you are middle-aged or older, you may need to invest more than 10%—maybe a lot more. Give the matter some careful thought and you will find a way. Even if you're over 50, you can still build wealth.

Compare yourself to the examples in chapter 8, find as close a match as you can, and start from there. Don't overlook all the assets that you have accumulated so far.

Study Your Assets

Go back to Form 2 in chapter 2, where you listed all your assets. Examine this list in light of what you know now.

First, look at all your liquid assets and investment assets. Are they properly invested? Are they working for you as hard as they can? Do you have two months' expenses in cash reserves? More? Less? Do you have some savings? Are they tax-free? Do you have an IRA or other qualified retirement account? Do you have enough life insurance? (See chapter 14.) Too much? Remember, life insurance won't make you rich. Are your mutual funds giving you at least 12% return per year? What are you earning in your IRA and other retirement plans?

Second, do you have assets that don't fit into your new wealth-building plan? Assets you don't use or don't need? For example, do you own an old car that doesn't run? A power mower or golf clubs you don't use? Do you rent a storage locker? What's in it? What about your attic? basement? garage? When you buy new clothes, what do you do with your old ones?

You can dispose of old items that you don't use anymore in two ways; sell them and add the cash to your investments (don't use it to buy more "stuff"), or donate them to charity and get a tax deduction. Deductions for gifts to charity can save you a significant amount of money on your tax bill. Gifts to recognized charities and religious groups are 100% deductible from income. If you give $1,000 worth of clothes and old furniture to charity, you reduce your income by $1,000 and hence save the tax on $1,000. That could be $200 to $400.

Third, what is missing from your list of assets? Do you need a lawn mower so you can cut your own grass and save the cost of a gardener? Do you need money in a tax-free bond fund? Do you need an IRA? Do you need to review your auto, home, health, and life insurance? Do you have disability insurance? While you are working, disability income protection insurance is more important than life insurance—much more. Just think for a moment. If you have life insurance and die, your family is taken care of. If you become disabled, they are not taken care of by your life insurance, and neither are you! You get nothing. Incidentally, you are 12 times more likely to be disabled for six months or more than to die during your working years.

Looking at your assets in this way will help you to focus everything on your plan. One reason you're not rich now may be because you never made these important choices before. You never focused on them and made them part of every decision you made. Now give them top priority. Make them part of every decision. Remember, this plan involves only about 10% of your income.

Look before You Buy

Are you buying a new car? Does it fit into your long-range plan? Could you buy a car that costs $30,000 instead of one that costs $40,000? Or one that costs $20,000 instead of $30,000? Think about it. It's one of the choices you have. If you can save $10,000, or any amount, by purchasing a less expensive car, put the money you save into your get-rich plan.

Are you going on vacation? Does it fit into your plan? Could you combine your vacation with business or family matters and thus combine two trips into one? Could you perhaps get tax deductions from the business trip? Could you go off-season for a lot less money? How many vacations have you had recently?

Are you redecorating? Does it fit into your plan? Does it increase the value of your home? Can you pay cash? Get a tax-deductible home equity loan? Get just a regular loan? Did you shop for the best deal? Do you have a firm price? Could you go over budget by $10,000? $20,000? Don't.

When you are shopping, do you shop with a list? For each purchase, ask, "Is it part of my budget?" What will you do with the old clothes, refrigerator, or other items you are replacing? Will you charge your purchases or pay cash? If you charge them, can you pay them off at the end of the month or interest-free period so you don't pay interest charges?

Look at what assets you have and apply these principles to your decisions about them. Use the tax laws. Plan for inflation and take advantage of it. Know the power of compound interest and invest in ownership, not loans. Certificates of deposit and savings accounts make bankers rich, not you.

Retirement Plans

An easy way to invest more than 10% without disturbing your budget at all is to put some of your income into a company-sponsored 401(k) or SEP-IRA or SAR-SEP-IRA plan. If your company offers such a plan, take maximum advantage of it. Here are three good reasons why you should:

1. Your contribution is 100% tax-deductible. If you put in $100 per month, that gives you a $1,200 deduction from income on line 24 or 27 of your 1040. If you saved $1,200 of your after-tax money and were in the 28% tax bracket, you would have to earn $1,666 and pay 28% in taxes, or $466 more, to have $1,200 left to invest.

   Looked at another way, your $1,200 investment costs you only $864 if you are in the 28% bracket because normally you would have to pay $336 in taxes on the $1,200 you earned. If your cost is $864 and your investment is worth $1,200, then you have made a return of $336 \times 864 = 38\%$ the first year, plus whatever interest or capital gains you make. Thirty-eight percent is a terrific rate of return. Do you know of any other investment from which you can make 38% every year? When you add your savings in state taxes, if any, the benefits to you are even greater.

2. Your earnings are tax-deferred. From now until you retire, you will not have to pay any taxes on your earnings. This can save you tens of thousands of dollars. Therefore, your retirement account will be tens of thousands of dollars larger than if you invested your personal money without this advantage of tax deferral.

3. Most companies make what is called a "company match" to 401(k) plans and SEP and SAR-SEP plans. This company match could be 25% or 50% or even 100% of the amount you contribute. Whatever it is, it is a tax-free gift to you. If you put in $1,200 and the company match is 50%, that means the company is giving you $600 a year, over and above your salary, tax-free. This is a *great* benefit.

These are three very important reasons to take advantage of these qualified plans. You have a choice. Each right choice uses the tax laws, and each can make you rich.

Extra Income

Another way to add to your wealth-building plan is to invest all the income you get in addition to your salary. Perhaps you have income from a personal loan you made to someone, a pension, or a disability payment. Add any additional income you may receive to your get-rich plan whenever you can. This is extra income, and it should be invested rather than spent. It will make your plan grow faster and help you retire sooner.

Another idea is to take the interest earned from a safe but low-paying fund or investment, such as a money market, municipal bond, or government bond fund, and add that interest to the growth investments in your get-rich fund. Most mutual fund companies will do this gladly at no charge. Just call and say that you want your interest deposited into your growth fund, whatever it is, each month.

Deposit monthly the interest from your bank savings accounts to your get-rich account. Every fund family will handle this for you. You'll be given a form to fill out and sign that authorizes your bank to send interest, either by check or wire, to your get-rich account. Total automatic deposits will be listed on your monthly statement, both from your bank and your fund(s). These deposits add up fast. They grow even faster!

If you're going to buy a house, consider where. Will you be able to walk to work? Drive to work? How far will you drive? Living close to where you work can save both time and money. Can you afford your mortgage? Can you pay it off quickly in 15 years or over only 30 years? Can you make extra payments from time to time? Extra payments on a regular basis can save you many thousands of dollars in interest and cut the length of your mortgage by many years. That's money in your pocket. The money saved on interest payments can be added to your investments when your mortgage is paid off early. Think about that carefully. Your mortgage interest is tax-deductible, which is a big benefit. On the other hand, getting rid of debt is part of a good plan. Certainly, when you retire you will want the mortgage to be paid off.

Refinancing

Are you thinking of refinancing your house? It's a good idea if it fits into your plan. Refinancing has three effects; most people look at only one.

1. Refinancing generally reduces monthly payments. Paying a reduced rate of interest or a reduced payment is a definite benefit to you. It helps your budget. It may give you extra money to add to your plan or help to pay college expenses.

   But look at the other two other effects of refinancing before you decide.

2. Refinancing can increase or decrease the size of your loan. There is a cost to refinancing a home. You can pay this extra cost out of pocket, or you can add it to the existing loan balance. If you do the latter, you will increase the size of your loan. This choice is counterproductive. Avoid it.

3. Refinancing can increase or decrease the term of the loan or the number of payments. If you have 25 years left on a 30-year loan and your new loan, with a lower interest rate and lower payments, is for 30 years again, you just went backward. If the new loan is for the same principal as the balance on the old one, you have just agreed to pay for your home for an extra five years. No wonder the banker loves you.

Ideally, when you refinance you should shorten the term, not extend it. If you can manage to pay for a 15-year loan to replace the 20 or 25 years left on an old 30-year loan, overall you will be *way* ahead. Your wealth plan will gain thousands of dollars. Figure out the difference using this template before you sign any papers for a new loan.

Table 11.1   Cost of Refinancing

Current Loan

Monthly payment = $ _____

Number of months left to pay it off _____

$ _____ × _____ = $ _____
  payment   no. of months   remaining cost
                                         of loan

New Loan

$ _____ × _____ = $ _____ + _____ =
  new payment   no. of months   cost of new   all closing costs
                                       loan   and points

$ _____
  grand total

If the total cost of your new loan, including points, refinance charges, and other charges, is more than the old one, it's not a good deal, or at least it won't help you get rich. A lower interest rate isn't the most important part of a loan. The *total cost to you* is the most important part if you want to be wealthy.

If the total cost of the new loan is $20,000 more than the old one and the new loan includes $20,000 in cash to add another bedroom, you've got a good deal. In fact, if you took out $20,000 in cash and if refinancing cost you only $40,000 over 15 or more years with the finance charges added in, that still could be a pretty good deal because you are borrowing at only 4.8% interest. That makes it very affordable.

Lower Payments Can Help—or Hurt

If you are refinancing your house so that you will have lower payments, so that you can put more money into building your wealth now, so that you will get the benefit of compound interest in your wealth plan for a longer period of time instead of waiting years until the mortgage is paid off, go to the head of the class. You get an A with a gold star.

Here's why: In today's market, you can borrow by using a home loan or home equity loan at 6% to 10% and then use the proceeds to invest and earn 12% or more. Your loan interest is tax-deductible because the loan is on your primary residence. This choice uses the tax laws to your advantage. The dollars you put into your investments now will compound over the full length of your mortgage, anywhere from 15 to 30 years. This uses the magic of compound interest. And you can invest tax-deferred, again using the tax laws.

For example, Charles is 40, his mortgage is $100,000 at 10% with 22 years left to go, and he decides to refinance it at 8-1/2% for 30 years. The new loan costs $2,800 in points and fees, which are added onto the remaining $100,000 balance.

Here is what that choice looks like: His original loan of 30 years at 10% will have had a total cost of $315,928, with monthly payments of $877.58. He has paid on it for 8 years, a total of $84,247. Over the next 22 years, he will pay a total of $231,681 more on his existing loan at 10%.

If he takes out a new 30-year loan for $102,800 ($100,000 + $2,800 in costs) at 8-1/2%, his monthly payments will be only $791.45. This is $86.43 less than the $877.58 he is paying on his present loan. This puts more money in his pocket every month, and this might be the only way he has to reduce his monthly expenses.

But look at the whole picture. He will make total payments of $284,922 to pay off the new loan over the next 30 years. The old one will cost him $231,681. Is the new loan worth this extra cost? It's the same house, after all. The old loan will be paid off when Charles is 62, just when he could start collecting Social Security if he were to retire then; the new one won't be paid off until age 70. That might prevent him from retiring early. It's essential to look at the whole picture and not spend a lot more than necessary.

Notice that borrowing money is expensive. When you are rich, you will be able to pay cash for a house like this and save all that interest. In fact, you will be earning interest on your wealth, not paying it. That way, you will be able to stay wealthy.

What should you do about cars and auto loans? Pay them off!

The following table shows the total cost to you, money out of your pocket, for a simple auto loan. It shows a $10,000 loan at 8%, 10%, 12%, or 14% that is paid off over three years, four years, five years, or six years.

Table 11.2   Cost of a $10,000 Auto Loan

	3-Year Loan	4-Year Loan	5-Year Loan	6-Year Loan
8%	$313.37	$244.13	$202.77	$177.86
	$11,281	$11,718	$12,166	$12,805
10%	$322.68	$253.63	$212.48	$188.04
	$11,616	$12,174	$12,748	$13,538
12%	$332.15	$263.34	$222.45	$198.61
	$11,957	$12,640	$13,347	$14,299
14%	$341.78	$273.27	$232.69	$209.63
	$12,304	$13,113	$13,961	$15,093

Note: The top line of each pair represents your monthly payment. The second line is your total cost.

Study the table for a few minutes. Notice that if you have good credit, then a simple $10,000 loan for three years at 8% (a very good rate) will cost you $313.37 per month for 36 months, or a total cost of $11,281. You will pay $1,281 for the privilege of borrowing $10,000. If your credit is not very good and you have to pay 14% interest, then your monthly payments will be $341.78, $28.41 more per month. This 14% loan will cost you a total of $12,304, rather than the $11,281 of the 8% loan. This is over $1,000 more for the same loan. Obviously, your good credit is valuable.

If you need the car and your credit is good, but you can't afford $313.37 per month, you could ask for a five-year loan, which reduces your monthly payment to only $202.77. However, this not only requires an additional two years of payments for the same car, it increases your total cost from $11,281 to $12,166, an extra $885 out of your pocket. If you stretch the loan out to six years, your payments drop to only $177.86 a month, but your total cost goes up to $12,805, an increase of over $1,500 on a $10,000 loan.

These changes in your monthly costs and total costs are very important to be aware of. In general, it is better to borrow less and pay it off sooner. But sometimes the lowest possible monthly payment is the most important aspect of a loan because you want to have money for other uses. Just understand that you will pay more in the long run if you reduce your monthly payments by stretching them out over a longer time.

The point is to look at the big picture. A lower interest rate isn't everything. A lower monthly payment isn't everything either. Be especially aware of leases. In a lease, you give up ownership and pay a middleman a profit. You may have somewhat lower payments, but your overall cost will be much more.

If you move or refinance your home, take out smaller and smaller loans for shorter and shorter periods of time. The rate of interest is *not* necessarily the critical feature. Sometimes the size of the monthly payment is the most important consideration. After all, the payment does have to fit into your monthly budget. Incidentally, many times auto companies offer special reduced rate financing of 2% to 3% during inventory clearance sales of last year's models in August and September and also during after-Christmas sales in January. This lower interest rate can save you money if you can negotiate a lower price, too. Many times, however, the auto dealer gives you a lower interest loan but won't discount or "deal" on the price. The dealer sells the car at full price.

A bank's biggest concern is not necessarily the rate of interest either. Banks want the loan so they can collect 8% to 10% from you on one hand and pay 2% to 4% interest to you on your savings on the other hand. Your strategy should be to reverse your position in this loser's game by borrowing as little as possible for as short a time as possible and investing for real gains of 12%, not just guaranteed accounts at 4%.

Chapter 12
Knowing's Not Enough: You Have to Work Your Plan

No one ever got rich by accident. A few people get rich by luck, by winning the lottery, for example, but even they had a plan: they bought a ticket! Do you wonder if they still have their money? Will you get rich? Will you be able to keep your money?

To answer yes to those last two questions requires a plan and a way to keep track of it. In this chapter you'll learn how to work your plan.

Your Income List

In chapter 2, you filled in two forms. On Form 1—Income you listed all of your income. The form includes your annual income from all sources—earned income, interest, dividends, and so on—and needs to be absolutely complete. It is for you only, as part of your plan to get rich. It's private. It's not for anyone else to see. You need to fill in a copy of this form every year and keep it in a file folder. You could easily do this when you prepare your tax return each year.

When you are rich, you will have a file of these forms for every year. Looking back through them will give you a simple, brief, and complete history of your rise to riches. When you are on your way there, looking over the forms will help show you what is working and what is not. It will take you an hour or two every year to complete this form, and the information will be an invaluable aid to you.

If you are working your plan properly, the income shown on the forms will change year by year. First of all, the total should go up every year. Your earned income from your jobs, which will be your biggest income when you start, should go up year by year. Gradually, your other incomes should go up, too.

The interest and dividends you earn should go up. This happens partly because you move your savings and investments to accounts that pay higher interest—from 2% money market accounts to 4% money market accounts, from no-interest checking accounts to interest-paying checking accounts, and from 4% CDs to 5.4% tax-free income funds—even if you have to change banks to do it.

Capital Gains

As you add more money every year to your investments, you earn more from them every year. Part of what you earn on your investments will be capital gains, so you will need a new category on Form 1 called "capital gains." (Note: A capital gain is the difference between what you paid for an investment and what you sold it for. If you bought stock for $4,000 and later sold it for $5,000, your capital gain would be $1,000. This is your profit and you are taxed on that profit. If you sold the stock for $3,500, you would have had a $500 capital loss.) Write down your capital gains for all accounts. Some years they will be a big boost to your wealth plan.

Taxable or Tax-deferred

You also need to note which income is taxable and which is not. You want to build the tax-free income and tax-deferred income with your new investment money. You should also convert as many investments as you can from taxable to tax favored, that is, either the income is tax-free or tax-deferred, or the purchase is tax-deductible as in an IRA or other qualified retirement plan.

Each of these steps will increase your income every year. You must record all income. Some of this income is usable and some is not. Some you may not think of as income—for example, the earnings in your IRA or other qualified retirement plan—but it is income and it's a definite part of your plan to get rich.

The income earned in your mutual funds, your annuities, your variable annuities, and every other investment you have must be recorded on the form every year. Even the income inside your IRA and other qualified retirement plans must be recorded. Even though you can't spend it and it's not taxable, you must record this income each year. This is one measure of the gain you have each year inside your plan.

This income record will show you, as the money grows, the power of investing. It will show you how money makes more money. It will show you the value of having money invested and the magic of compound interest. It will also show you that you are moving ahead toward your goal and that your goal is attainable. It will reinforce your desire to be rich!

Keep these records of your earned income year by year, study them, and you will be successful. Also use them to teach your children how money works. Then they can be successful, too.

Your Asset List

The second form you filled out in chapter 2 was a list of your assets. You also studied that in chapter 8. Now you need a second kind of asset list. You can use the one from chapter 2 to list your personal property assets. These are the "things" you own: your home, other real estate including land, cars, trucks, RVs, boats, art, collections, antiques, tools and equipment, furniture and electronics, patents, copyrights, and all other objects of value or significance.

These items are your nonworking assets. They are not part of your plan to get rich. They can be useful and have real value. If they don't, get rid of them. Keeping this first list will make you aware of how you spend your money. You used some of your money to buy these items. Was that a good use of your money or not? Wasting money will *not* make you rich.

When you buy something significant that should be listed on your asset list, just write it in, including the date of purchase and cost. When you sell or dispose of an asset on this list, cross it out and put down the date and how much you sold it for or what happened to it.

This is a very simple record, kept year by year. The point is to stay aware of what you own and why. You also must be aware of the value of what you own. Are your possessions going up in value or down? Do you own more or the same?

Do you need to buy something to improve the list? Should you get rid of some items, either sell them or give them away? Do you need to replace an old item with a newer one? Remember that gifts to charities can make very nice tax deductions.

Investment Assets

The following new assets list is for your investment assets only. As part of your wealth-building plan, you need to keep a record of your investments and their value. Use this investment assets form to list your investments by categories: cash reserves, fixed-rate accounts, and growth accounts.

Form 3   Investment Assets (Ownership)

Do not list nonprofitable or illiquid assets here. They are listed on Form 2—Assets.

(Do not write here yet)	Number	Total Value
Cash Reserves		
___ Checking accounts	___	$ _____
___ Money market accounts	___	_____
___ Savings accounts	___	_____
Total		$ _____
Fixed-Rate Accounts		
___ Qualified plans	___	$ _____
___ Certificates of deposit	___	_____
___ Fixed annuities	___	_____
___ Municipal bonds or funds	___	_____
___ Corporate bonds or funds	___	_____
___ Government bonds or funds	___	_____
___ Life insurance cash value	___	_____
___ Other	___	_____
Total		$ _____
Growth Accounts		
___ Qualified plans	___	$ _____
___ Stocks or stock funds	___	_____
___ International stocks or funds	___	_____

___ Specialty stocks or funds	___	_____
___ Variable annuities	___	_____
___ Variable life	___	_____
___ Options	___	_____
___ Futures	___	_____
___ Liquid income property	___	_____
___ Other	___	_____
Total		$ _____
Total of all investments		$ _____

Four Questions

Ask yourself these questions once a year when you make this list:
- Are your investments on track to make you rich?
- Should any of them be sold?
- Which ones should you be adding to?
- Are you getting all the tax benefits you can from them?

Some of these investments will be in IRAs and other qualified retirement plans; some will be your personal nonqualified investments. Some will be tax-sheltered; some will not.

The value of the items on this list should grow rapidly, first, because you are adding to them it regularly, and second, because your investments are each growing in value. The sole purpose of investing is to own assets—in this case, stocks, mutual funds, real estate—that will increase in value. This annual checkup will quickly tell you if you are being successful.

You must prune your investments just as a gardener prunes vines and trees, and you must add to and fertilize them also. This is good management. Get rid of the losers and add to the ones that show good growth. If you're not sure about how to do this, get advice from a good certified financial planner or other professional.

Don't be emotional about your investments, and don't hang on to one just because you bought it or, even worse, because you inherited it. Examine inherited investments very carefully. Be sure they are working for you now. Just because they worked for your grandpa and your dad doesn't mean they are right for you. Sell them if they don't fit your plan, and put the proceeds into what *you* need. Here's a point to remember about inheritances. When you inherit something—shares of stock, real estate, or whatever—for tax purposes its "cost" to you is its value on the day your benefactor died. If a stock was valued at $100 a share the day you inherited it, that is your cost. Your dad may have bought it at $20 a share, and perhaps he was reluctant to sell it and pay the taxes on that $80 profit per share. You, however, can sell it now at $100 and pay no taxes because your cost was $100. You have *no* profit in it. Therefore, you may be better off selling the stock now (especially if you don't know much about the company's future prospects), buying a mutual fund, and letting the fund manager look out for your investment.

Also don't worry about past mistakes—a stock you invested in that went down in value or a fund you could have invested in, but didn't, that went up. Take care of what you have now. Learn from the past and then forget it.

Review your investment list annually. Take a few hours once a year to update your list. Do it carefully and accurately. Mark the investment assets that are taxable and those that are not. Make separate totals for each and figure the grand total of both categories.

Study the current year's investment assets list and review the previous years' lists. The investments should be growing faster and faster. If they are, this will tell you that your plan is working and demonstrate to you the power that is building in your plan. You will see that you are building wealth, that you are succeeding, that you are going to be rich.

Chapter 13
When Things Go Wrong

In the examples so far, all went smoothly and the investors reached their financial goals right on schedule. That happens for a great many people, and it can happen for you, too. But sometimes events don't go the way you had planned.

Sandy's husband died at age 48. Dr. Dave got divorced at 45. You could get laid off and be out of a job tomorrow. An accident could leave you needing a large amount of cash. Whatever the disaster, your plan can help.

If Your Income Stops

Building financial wealth depends on income and a steady flow of contributions into your various investments. If your income stops for any reason, your contributions must stop.

Your cash reserves, developed in step 1 in the financial planning process, are there to carry you for three months and maybe more. Use them first. If you were laid off and you received severance pay, you can use that money. If there was a death, use the life insurance proceeds. Use the savings and investments that pay the lowest interest and rate of return first. *Do not cash in IRA or qualified retirement plans*. They should be earning the highest rates of return, *and* you will incur large tax penalties for cashing in these qualified plans before age 59.5. Use CDs and personal accounts first.

Depending on your situation, you may need to consider borrowing money for living expenses. Look for loans in this order:

1. A home equity loan with tax-deductible interest
2. A personal or signature loan, which is simple and easy
3. A cash advance on your credit cards, which has the highest interest

If your income stops, use debt as a last resort and use it sparingly.

The Unexpected—Accidents

An accident occurs. Suddenly you need cash—a large amount of cash—maybe $10,000 or more.

First, remember that insurance is designed to provide cash to cover most unexpected events. Your auto insurance should cover the cost of all car accidents. Your health insurance should cover at least 80% of all medical expenses for you and your family. Your homeowner's policy should cover the cost of all accidents in your home or damage to your home by any covered cause. Your disability insurance should provide you with an income when you are too sick to work. All this is true in theory. In real life, however, sometimes you discover after an accident happens that your insurance doesn't cover it.

Cash in Your Lowest-Earning Accounts First

When you need $10,000 now, the process is the same as when your income stops: start with your cash reserves. How much do you have there?

Next look at bank CDs, municipal bonds, and other personal savings accounts. These generally earn less than your stock and mutual funds, so they should be cashed in first.

After that, go to your personal investments: stocks, bonds, and mutual funds. Some of these should have taxable long-term capital gains in them. So first take the ones that will cost the least in taxes. For example, a stock or fund that has gone up 10% in value should normally be sold before one that has increased 40% in value.

Avoid using any qualified plan assets for two reasons:

1. All money coming out of a qualified plan is taxable, and you will pay penalties for withdrawing money before you are age 59.5.
2. These are your main wealth-building assets. They depend on the magic of compound interest every year, and that cannot be replaced. You are reducing your wealth and your retirement when you take money out of your retirement plans prematurely.

Finally, if you don't have the money you need readily available in one of your accounts, borrow it. Here are some possibilities:

1. A short-term signature loan from your bank for a few months or one or two years. No collateral is required, just your signature.
2. A home equity loan for any length of time and for larger amounts.
3. Other secured loans, that is, where you have to put up collateral to back the loan.
4. Cash advances against your credit cards. These are probably the most expensive loans, so these should be your last choice.

Whatever your situation, remember and use the basic keys to building wealth:

- Ownership. Think long and hard before you sell an asset that is part of your wealth-building plan.

- Compound interest. Keep high-performance funds and stocks. Don't interrupt that compound growth. You can never replace it.
- Taxes. Beware of taxes when you sell a financial asset. Nonfinancial assets such as art, jewelry, cameras, and old autos can sometimes be sold without any tax consequences.

Restart Your Plan

When the emergency is over and the problem solved, go right back to your wealth-building plan, following the seven-step process. You may have lost a little ground, but restart your plan. You may have to reduce your contributions for a while. That's okay. Just invest as much as you can. All the long-range benefits are still there and working for you.

Adjust the numbers in your plan to take into account your new circumstances. You may have lower income (or higher) or you may have new loan payments to make. Whatever your situation, don't quit!

Part 4
A Closer Look at the Seven-Step Process

You've seen how others have gone from having almost nothing to building wealth. The next chapters provide details on how to use the financial planning process and explains why it works. You'll see how success, wealth, and retirement can be yours, and you'll learn how to provide a proper estate for your heirs.

Chapter 14
Cash Reserves and Insurance: Steps 1 and 2

Cash reserves start with the extra dollars in your checking account, then include regular deposits in a money market fund and a tax-free bond fund. These are discussed in chapter 8. They are liquid reserves that you can access everyday for unexpected events and small emergencies. They generally should be equal to one to three months' household expenses.

The seven steps are listed in the order of priority, so you start with a cash reserve, no matter how small. Then as you accumulate assets you insure them—car, home, and others. That first insurance premium is paid from the cash reserve in your checkbook. Next, you start saving and investing, and those first contributions come out of current income and your cash reserves.

After you have money flowing into your insurance, savings, and investments, you do longer range planning and refine your efforts with more specific tax, retirement, and estate planning.

———

Probably nothing in the world of finance is more boring than insurance. The thought of having to spend time discussing insurance, thinking about car crashes and hospital bills and death and estate taxes, can be just plain depressing! This is especially true when insurance agents pull out charts and graphs showing just how awful it is going to be for you without insurance. But, of course, everything will be okay if you'll just sign the papers and write a check to "The Friendly Insurance Company," and another one next month and the next month and every month after that, too. "We will take care of you," says the agent.

However, *you* have to take care of you.

To do this doesn't require becoming an insurance expert. It just requires common sense. There are three basic things you're paying for when you purchase an insurance policy. Just keep them in mind, ask the right questions, and make sure you are getting what you want.

1. Cost (How much are the premiums?)
2. Claims payment (How quickly are claims paid? How easy is the claims process?)
3. Benefits (What areas and items are covered?)

Casualty Insurance

Casualty insurance, which includes auto and homeowner's insurance, is less complicated than life or health or disability insurance, so let's look at it first.

Auto Insurance

Assume you buy your first car when you are 20 and you will drive until you are 85. If your auto policy premium costs are $1,000 per year, then over the next 65 years you will spend $65,000 for auto insurance. If you could get the same coverage and same value at another company for $900 per year, then your lifetime cost would be $58,500. That $6,500 savings is a lot of money. If premium rates go up 3% a year, and they well might, then the first auto insurance policy will cost you about $155,000 over your lifetime. The $900 policy will cost about $137,000, a savings of $18,000.

If your insurance starts at $1,500 per year because you drive newer, sportier, more expensive cars, then it could cost you $232,400. If you have two cars, it will cost you about 50% more than the cost for just one car. This would be $1,500 per year for two standard cars, two years old, or about $2,250 for newer, sportier cars.

Table 14.1   Auto Insurance Cost over a Lifetime of Driving (65 Years), Age 20 to 85

	Company A Cost per Year	Lifetime Cost	Company B Cost per Year	Lifetime Cost	10% Savings
Standard car, 2 years old	$1,000	$65,000	$900	$58,500	$6,500
3% inflation	0	155,000	0	137,000	18,000
New sports car or two standard, older cars	$1,500	$97,500	$1,350	$87,750	$9,750
3% inflation	0	232,400	0	209,200	23,200
2-car family	$2,250	$146,220	$2,075	$131,600	$14,625
3% inflation	0	348,500	0	313,600	34,900

So cost is critically important. Over the course of your life, you are going to spend a lot of money on auto insurance. Therefore, you have to shop and compare. Does this mean you should buy the cheapest policy? No. You should buy the policy with the best value.

What do you want for your money? It's simple: a company that will pay you and pay you promptly without a lot of runaround or haggling when you have a claim. You want the service you rightly deserve since you paid for it.

Ask your friends, ask everyone you see at work or at your clubs and groups, who their insurance carrier is and what they think of the company. Why do they like it? Did they shop around? Also go to the reference desk at the library. Find out how insurance companies are rated and then call three good ones and have them give you proposals. Many large, well-known companies have excellent claims-paying records and good service. That is what you are buying, good value. It is always worth it to pay a little more, not a lot more, to get good service when you need it. If you're sure you'll never have a claim, absolutely positive, then the cheapest policy will do. But if someone skids into your car one rainy night, you will want service.

Benefits are what you receive if your claim is upheld. If you can't afford to spend $3,000 to $10,000 or more right now because someone crashes into your car or you are involved in a big accident of any kind or your car is stolen, then you need the coverage that will take care of these emergencies. You need the right benefits, tailored to your needs. On your auto policy, you'll need coverage for fire and theft, collision, comprehensive, uninsured motorist, and towing, at a minimum. You need high coverage, of at least 5 to 10 times your income. This is so that if you get sued after an accident, your insurance will protect you. If a person has $50,000 in medical expenses because of an accident you were involved in, he or she could well sue you for $250,000 for expenses, loss of income, pain and suffering, and more. Three people were in the car, you'd better have a lot of insurance. The higher your income and apparent wealth, the more you will be sued for. There is no point in having a good insurance policy at a good company at a fair price if you wind up paying half the damages yourself because you didn't cover all the risks.

Be cost conscious. Use a good company. Get the proper coverage. It will keep your finances from being wiped out or at least prevent your having to pay a big claim and/or expenses out of your pocket. The right coverage keeps your retirement money securely working in your investment plan. It means you stay on schedule to get rich regardless of the inevitable turns in the road. You are protected; therefore, you will succeed.

Homeowner's Insurance

Your homeowner's insurance works the same way as your auto insurance. You want to pay a fair price for the exact coverage you need, not necessarily the cheapest price. You want your policy with a strong company that will pay when you have a claim, and you want complete coverage.

Your home may be your biggest asset; you certainly want to protect it, its contents, and the people who come and go on your property. You are liable for any calamities that may befall people while they are there. Be prepared and be protected. Your home is valuable, and if you are going to be rich, you must take care of it and protect it. If it needs a new roof, you have to provide it. If it burns or a guest falls and is injured, you need insurance to pay for the damages, without interrupting your wealth-building plan.

Talk to friends and shop around. An auto insurer often offers a special discounted package if you have both your auto and homeowner's insurance with the company. Find out.

Don't get less than the full coverage you need or you will be cheating yourself. You must insure your home for its current replacement cost. If you bought your home ten years ago for $100,000 and insured it for that amount and today it is worth $150,000, you have to increase your insurance to $150,000. If you don't and your house burns down, the insurance company will pay you only $100,000, not the $150,000 you need to replace the house. The company will use the same ratio of *replacement cost* in paying your other claims, too. In this example, therefore, it will only pay two-thirds of most claims (100,000:150,000 = 2:3).

Your homeowner's policy should include the following:

- *Comprehensive coverage,* which covers damage to the building and its contents (up to 70% of the value of the dwelling) due to fire, smoke, water, rain, wind, collapse, vandalism, and so on. Flood insurance is available only through the U.S. government; earthquake insurance is available as an option at an extra cost.

- *Theft,* which covers your personal property at home, anywhere while traveling, or in your car. Items worth more than $500, such as cameras, stamp or coin collections, fine art, jewelry, sports equipment, guns, securities, and silverware should be covered by an additional personal articles floater policy.

- *Personal Liability Protection,* which pays for bodily injuries to other people or damage to their property, if you are liable, resulting from

- Unintentional acts committed by qualified family members, including hunting, fishing, and other sporting activities
- The acts of your pets

This coverage also pays the medical expenses for other people accidentally injured through your activities regardless of liability.

- Finally, *An umbrella policy,* issued by the same company that carries your homeowner's coverage, which augments the underlying liability provided by your auto and homeowners insurance and will protect your assets in any form. This also includes coverage against libel, slander, defamation of character, and other similar charges.

Health Insurance

Next in order of importance is health insurance. Most employers offer health insurance as an employee benefit. The insurance is a group plan and is generally considerably less expensive than an individual plan. If it is a good plan, take as much coverage as you can get. If your employer pays all of the cost, great! If you have to pay some or even all of the cost, it's probably still a good deal. The way to find out for sure, of course, is to research the plan. Get a complete list of all the benefits provided.

A good health plan covers all basic hospital and doctor costs plus some or all of these extra services: prescription drugs, x-rays, dental care, eye care, chiropractic care, alternative medicine, mental health services, and home care.

Two common types of health policies are available now: HMO (health maintenance organization)/managed care and PPO (preferred provider organization), a more individually controlled program. You may pay a deductible amount from $250 to $2,000 before you can collect anything from the insurer. Then there is an 80/20, 70/30 or 60/40 copayment period where you pay 20%, 30%, or 40% and the insurance company pays 80%, 70%, or 60% of covered medical costs. If your costs reach the stop-loss amount of $5,000 to $10,000, which is the maximum you would pay for any one sickness or accident or in any one year, the insurance company pays any additional costs.

Most policies now consist of a small copayment for each office visit, plus you pay a percentage of the total cost of the visit and extra services provided, such as lab tests and x-rays. This same percentage applies to your hospital costs.

Have your health insurance agent go over each of these items with you so you understand both the cost to you of the insurance policy and the cost you will pay for all doctor visits, doctor services, lab services, hospital stays, and other services. In other words, how much of each of these expenses will you pay and how much will the insurance company pay? If you are on a budget, the trick is to balance the known cost of the insurance with the unknown cost of actual healthcare needed.

Now start shopping. See what it would cost for the same level of coverage from good companies for an individual policy. Study the benefits offered and see if they are sufficient. See if the coverage is too low; perhaps the company's policy pays only 50% of expenses and you need 80% or more. Or maybe it has a $2,500 deductible and you want an $800 deductible. Compare costs and benefits. If the benefits in the policy offered by your company are too skimpy, you might be better off not enrolling in the plan and buying your own insurance. However, even if the benefits are skimpy, if the policy is paid for 100% by the company, you should probably enroll. Maybe you can find an inexpensive supplemental health plan to cover the gaps.

Disability Insurance

Life insurance and disability insurance are a little different. Disability insurance pays you if you can't work because you become physically ill or disabled. If you are lying in a hospital or nursing home or recovering from an illness or accident at home, your health insurance policy pays the hospital and all of your doctors, but who pays you? Your disability policy pays you when you can't work. Whether your disability is a temporary condition of three to six months or a year or a lifetime condition because of a permanent disability, your disability insurance policy pays you so you can buy food and clothes for yourself and your family, and it provides the income you need to pay your mortgage on time.

Disability insurance is different from property insurance because you and your body are not the same as a car. Therefore, it's critical that you understand the terms of the policy and the conditions under which you can collect. You must shop for policies and compare them carefully. Fortunately, relatively few companies offer such policies: UNUM, Transamerica, and American Travelers are three good companies to look at.

Here again, you are buying benefits for yourself and your family, so get good value. If you can't work you want to be paid for as long as you can't work. You will also need to be paid if you can work only part-time as you are recovering from an accident or illness or if you can never work full-time again. A good disability policy will take care of you when you need to be taken care of. That's what you are paying for. That's what you need.

Life Insurance

Life insurance is often thought of as a tough subject. No one wants to discuss death, especially one's own. So we won't discuss it here. Instead, we'll discuss life because life insurance, if it is needed, can be bought as an investment to enhance your living, not your dying. Make it part of your investment program. It can add substantially to your get-rich plan now and when you retire and serve your heirs and estate, too.

First of all, you don't need life insurance unless you have financial dependents, people who are dependent on you for financial support. Dependents commonly include young children and their mother, a nonworking spouse, or retired parents with little or no income. If some or all of these people are dependent on you for their income, then your disability income and life insurance must properly provide for them. It is the least expensive and most cost-efficient way to take care of these financial responsibilities. These two types of insurance will keep you and/or your spouse from becoming poor. Being poor is not in your plan! Your plan is to be rich.

If you don't have financial dependents, don't buy life insurance. You don't need it. Who would be the beneficiary? The rule in buying any kind of insurance is to use your common sense. If you are 25 or 45 or 65 and single, never married, with no children and with parents who are doing fine, why do you need life insurance? Take the money you would have spent on the insurance and put it into a variable annuity.

A woman once told me she was planning to buy a car in about six months (she didn't own one at the time), and she wondered if she should buy the auto insurance now because it might be cheaper before her next birthday. The answer, of course, is no. You don't buy insurance until you need it.

There are two exceptions to this rule, which we will cover in detail later in this chapter. One is to provide tax-free income during retirement; the other is to pay estate taxes in large estates.

Remember Sandy in chapter 1? She was married at 25, and when she became pregnant with her first child, her husband, Jim, 28, took out a $100,000 life insurance policy on himself. It seemed like an awful lot of insurance at the time, and it really squeezed their budget, but they had a need and he insisted. After they had three children, $100,000 didn't seem like too much insurance, but they never bought more. When he died at 48, Sandy wished that somehow they had forced themselves to buy more.

She was grateful for the $100,000 insurance proceeds, however. She used some of it to help pay Jim's final expenses, some of it helped their two youngest children with college expenses, and the rest went into her investment accounts, which were pretty simple. Sandy had her IRA that she had added to faithfully every year, plus Jim's IRA, and $11,000 in the bank. Within two years, Sandy had to reroof the house and paint it, and she used quite a bit more of Jim's insurance money for that.

Sandy had to go back to work after her husband died, and she got along all right. But if Sandy and Jim had reexamined their need for life insurance after their third child was born, they would have easily seen that he needed at least $400,000 of life insurance to protect Sandy and the girls in the event of his death. Jim died when their two younger daughters were still in college. If he had died ten years sooner, or even five, it would have driven his family's standard of living way down. Sandy would have had to go back to work while the children were still in elementary school, and it would have been a real struggle even to keep the house.

How Much Do You Need?

How do you determine how much life insurance a person needs? There are three simple ways:

1. Ten times your income. If you have a high income and want to provide for your beneficiary so that person will never have to work and will always be financially independent, then purchase life insurance equal to 10 times your income. If you earn $70,000 a year, then get a $700,000 policy. This could provide a lifetime income to your survivor of about $60,000 a year, which should be adequate.

   Of course, if you purchase 12 times or 15 times your income, your survivor could have an even higher lifetime income and standard of living. However, your cost will go up, too, and the policy may become too expensive, not an efficient use of money.

2. Five times your income. This is a simple, reasonable, and generally affordable way to calculate the amount of life insurance to carry to protect a family. If you earn $40,000 a year, then five times that amount, which is a $200,000 life insurance policy, is affordable and is probably enough to cover the basic needs of your dependents. It may not be enough to cover the children's college expenses, however.

3. Practical method. This is an easy method used to calculate how much life insurance is needed. It shows in a simple way the amount of cash your heirs will need to continue the same lifestyle in the same house and neighborhood they live in now if you are not there bringing in your income. If you don't want your family to have to move away from the neighborhood you picked out— your home, friends, schools, and church—because you died young, then this is one way to provide for them.

List these expenses and add them up:

1. Two years' income $_____
2. Home mortgage (balance you owe)   _____
3. Other debt   _____
4. Final expenses (estimate)   _____
5. Children's college costs   _____
   (list for each child)   _____

                                                         _____
6. Other family plans, including   _____
   school for the survivor, cottage,   _____
   big vacation, RV, boat, other   _____

   Total $_____

Here is how this method works. In this example, for simplicity, the surviving spouse is a woman. However, the same rules apply for both women and men. If the woman provides income for the family, it needs to be replaced in the same way.

1. Two years' income. This enables your survivor to live for two years without having to work at a job while she puts her life back together, while she and the children learn how to live without you. She could decide to move back to her hometown or go back to school to learn new skills. It gives her freedom to build a new future.

2. Home mortgage. This is a fixed cost and should be payable in advance. Your widow now can live in your home, the one you chose together, for the rest of her life, rent-free. It is paid for. This will help her get by on a lower income because she doesn't have to pay the mortgage. She will still have to pay the taxes and homeowner's insurance, however.

3. Other debt. The money allotted for this item will pay all your debts so your widow can live in your house with your children debt-free. She could go back to school to sharpen her skills and go to work within two years and continue to live just the way you both lived together. Without debt or mortgage payments, she could probably earn enough to support the children and herself there.

4. Final expenses. You don't want your heirs to go into debt to pay your funeral and burial costs. You provide for them in advance. These expenses range from

the simplest embalming or cremation and burial for $1,000 to a small coffin and memorial service for $5,000 or a large service held for a large number of people for $10,000 or more.

5. Children's college costs. If you had planned to help pay for your children's college expenses, then you must provide for that. These costs keep going up, so figure some inflation in this, perhaps 3% or even 6%. If your children will live at home and go to local public colleges, then perhaps $5,000 a year for tuition, books, transportation, and other expenses is reasonable. If they will be going away to a large public university, figure $15,000 a year or more. A private school such as Harvard or Stanford will cost closer to $40,000 a year, plus the increase per year due to inflation. Your local library has books that can give you a lot of help in figuring college costs. So do the major brokerage houses and most investment counselors.

6. Other family plans. These are purchases you had always expected to make for your family and that you want to carry through on. These could include a vacation home, ski equipment for everybody, a sailboat, or a vacation in Spain. If something is an important part of your family's plan, then write it down and attach a dollar value to it. Include education plans for the survivor here, also.

Now add all these amounts together and write in the total. That is how much it would reasonably cost your widow or survivor to carry on alone, without you and your income. This is the minimum amount of insurance you'll need.

You are worth a lot more than your income, of course, but we have no way to replace you as a human being. Your income can be replaced, however, with life insurance.

Even for a nonworking spouse, final expenses must be paid, and life insurance is the best and cheapest way to pay them.

The purpose of life insurance is to protect your family and what you are building and to enable those around you to continue living comfortably and to keep building. It has a cost, and all the factors in your wealth-building plan must be balanced; insurance is just one part of any plan to get rich.

Go back to chapter 8 and reread the three illustrations there. Insurance is the second step in the seven-step financial planning process, and the three illustrations all include the appropriate amount of life insurance for three families of different incomes—$40,000, $70,000, and $120,000 per year. The life insurance is paid for out of the 10% of income used to build their wealth.

Reread chapter 9, which gives illustrations of building wealth starting at ages 25, 35, and 45. Life insurance is an integral part of all these plans.

If you need $300,000 of protection and you have $300,000 in cash, excluding retirement funds, then you don't need any life insurance. You have the cash to provide what is needed. If you already have a good policy for $100,000, then you need only an additional $200,000 worth of insurance. If you have $50,000 in mutual funds, then you need only $250,000 in life insurance to provide the $300,000 needed by your dependents.

Do not count any retirement money, IRAs, 401(k)s, or other company retirement plans of any kind as part of the money needed to support your family and replace your income. The life insurance is in case you die now. If you don't, *you* will need to use your retirement funds. Keep them for your retirement. Life insurance provides money to live on now. You and your family need both.

Life insurance, bought to protect your family, must always be *whole life, universal life, or variable life, never term life*. It needs to be permanent insurance with cash value—the more cash value the better.

Whole Life Insurance

Whole life is life insurance with a fixed cost—premium—that you pay for over your whole lifetime. The policy builds a pool of cash value because the fixed premium is more than the cost of the insurance in the early years when you are younger. This pool then defers part of the higher cost when you are older and paying less than the actual cost of the life insurance. This cash value also earns a little interest, so it keeps growing. The cash value grows tax-free, and because it is part of the policy, it belongs to you. Therefore, the insurance company will let you borrow it. Any such loan is tax-free (as all loans are), and the company will charge you interest on these loans. The better companies, however, will charge you the same interest they are paying you on the cash value buildup, so it is a "wash loan"—that is, there is no cost to you. These loans don't have to be paid back, and in the case of "wash loans," the cash value can keep growing.

This cash value is available to you, but it does not belong to you. When you die, the insurance company pays out the death benefit and keeps the cash value. Therefore, if you borrow against the cash value, it reduces the death benefit of the policy. In effect, the insurance company pays off the loan from the death benefit, then pays your heirs the remainder.

In spite of this, the cash value is a very useful tool and fits very nicely into a good financial plan.

Universal Life Insurance

Universal life is a greatly improved version of whole life. The interest paid on the cash value in a whole life policy is usually quite low. Universal life, developed almost 30 years ago, pays a higher market rate of interest. This makes the cash value grow faster. After a certain number of years, the interest earned on the cash value is often enough to pay the premium! The policy is then called "paid up."

A whole life policy is designed to be paid up at age 99. Universal life can be paid up in 10 years, 20 years, at age 65, or whatever you choose. These policies allow you to pay extra toward the premium—to overpay—to build up the cash value quickly so that the policy becomes paid up at an early age. If it is paid up when you retire, then not only do your expenses go down, but you have another asset—the tax-free cash value—to draw on if needed.

The interest rate paid into the cash value fluctuates with market interest rates. This sometimes can be a problem. If rates go down, the cash value may not earn enough to pay the premium. If this happens after the policy is paid up, then it is no longer paid up, and you have to start paying premiums again. If the policy is not paid up when rates go down, it means you will have to continue paying premiums longer than you had anticipated. Because of this, premiums and cash values are *not* guaranteed in a universal life policy. Both *are* guaranteed in a whole life policy but are generally higher than for a universal life policy.

Variable Life Insurance

Variable life is a universal life policy with one big change. Instead of paying interest on the cash value, the insurance company offers you a choice of several mutual funds to invest in. The hope here is that the funds will grow at a much higher rate, perhaps 12%, than the interest normally paid, perhaps 6%. This introduces an element of risk to the buyer but also a chance for his or her money to grow faster.

During retirement, this cash value can be used as retirement income. A $300,000 policy that you have been paying into for 30 years or more could easily have a cash value of $100,000–$150,000. In many cases, you could borrow $10,000 a year from this policy for 25 years or more and use it as income during your retirement. Remember, the loans don't have to be paid back. The policy continues to receive interest and dividends, paid by the insurance company, so the cash value is being added to even while you are taking cash out in the form of loans. These loans are tax-free, just like any other loan. (When you borrow $10,000 from your bank, you don't pay taxes on the money you receive, just interest on the loan.) So these loans can provide tax-free income to you in your retirement. Tax-free income is the best kind of income you can have.

———

For family protection, you need cash value life insurance, either whole life, universal life, or variable life—not term life. The level premium, the cash value, and the ability to pay up the policy, that is, to have it fully paid for in 15 or 20 years or at age 65, are the reasons why you should always use cash value insurance for family protection. Term insurance has no cash value and therefore can never be paid up.

Term Life Insurance

Term life insurance is used in certain situations where you have a specific risk for only a fixed period of time. For example, if you just changed jobs and are planning to retire in 10 years and your new company doesn't offer any life insurance, you might take out a 10-year term policy to protect your spouse until you reach retirement age and are eligible for your pension and other retirement income. Often an auto loan will have term insurance attached to it to pay off the loan if you should die before it is fully paid. Most home mortgages have term life insurance attached to them. Term insurance works where the period of risk is strictly limited. One-, two-, or three-year policies are common, enough to pay off a loan or perhaps for living overseas on assignment for a year or two. Ten- to fifteen-year terms are also common and are used to fill the gap until retirement, until a debt or mortgage is paid off, or until an investment matures.

Sometimes term insurance is all that can be afforded. Then it is better than nothing, but if the insurance is needed long term for family protection, term insurance is a poor substitute for all the benefits of good cash value insurance. Term should be replaced with cash value insurance as soon as possible. Also, the cost of term insurance keeps going up, while whole life costs are guaranteed and universal life costs are fairly level and fixed.

Other Reasons for Life Insurance

Two other reasons for having a large life insurance policy, other than for family protection, are

1. As a source of tax-free income during retirement
2. As a way to reduce estate taxes by up to 90% in large estates of $2,000,000 or more

Tax-Free Retirement Income

Dr. Dave, mentioned in chapter 1, was 45 when his divorce was final and he started over financially. One of his first investments was a $1,000,000 life insurance policy, and he put as much cash as he could into it. In his case, it was $30,000 a year. Why did he do that? He did it for additional tax-free retirement income.

He had a Keogh plan at his office that provided some retirement benefits for him and his full-time nurse and receptionist. He contributed $26,400 a year to the plan: $18,000 for himself, $6,000 for his nurse, and $2,400 for the receptionist. At best, this might grow to $1,450,000 by age 65, which could give him a fully taxable income then at 6% interest, of about $87,000 a year. He wants more than that. That's where his new insurance policy comes in. The table below shows what he is doing.

Table 14.2 Premiums and Withdrawals from a Typical Universal Life or Whole Life Policy

Yr.	Age	Premium Outlay $	Partial Withdrawal $	Net Loan $	Annual Net Outlay $	Accum. Value Less Loans $	Cash Surrender Value $	Death Benefit $
1	45	30,000	0	0	30,000	24,831	12,984	583,675
2	46	30,000	0	0	30,000	51,412	40,881	610,255
3	47	30,000	0	0	30,000	79,975	70,660	638,719
4	48	30,000	0	0	30,000	110,384	102,485	669,227
5	49	30,000	0	0	30,000	143,103	136,521	701,946
6	50	30,000	0	0	30,000	178,205	172,940	737,045
7	51	30,000	0	0	30,000	215,871	211,922	774,715
8	52	30,000	0	0	30,000	256,281	253,648	815,124
9	53	30,000	0	0	30,000	299,631	298,315	858,475
10	54	30,000	0	0	30,000	346,112	346,112	904,955
Total		300,000			300,000			
11	55	30,000	0	0	30,000	400,454	400,454	959,297
12	56	30,000	0	0	30,000	458,732	458,732	1,017,575
13	57	30,000	0	0	30,000	521,220	521,220	1,020,062
14	58	30,000	0	0	30,000	588,076	588,926	1,146,870
15	59	30,000	0	0	30,000	659,437	659,437	1,218,281
16	60	30,000	0	0	30,000	735,727	735,727	1,294,570
17	61	30,000	0	0	30,000	817,399	817,399	1,376,242
18	62	30,000	0	0	30,000	904,828	904,828	1,463,671
19	63	30,000	0	0	30,000	998,422	998,422	1,557,265
20	64	30,000	0	0	30,000	1,098,641	1,098,641	1,657,484
Total		600,000	0	0	600,000			

*A zero in the premium outlay column does not mean the policy is paid up. Charges will continue to be deducted from the accumulated value as long as the policy remains inforce. Additional premium outlays may be necessary.

Yr.	Age	Premium Outlay $	Partial Withdrawal $	Net Loan $	Annual Net Outlay $	Accum. Value Less Loans $	Cash Surrender Value $	Death Benefit $
21	65	0	90,000	0	−90,000	1,081,241	1,081,241	1,567,484
22	66	0	90,000	0	−90,000	1,062,697	1,062,697	1,477,484
23	67	0	90,000	0	−90,000	1,042,993	1,042,993	1,387,484
24	68	0	90,000	0	−90,000	1,022,124	1,022,124	1,297,484
25	69	0	90,000	0	−90,000	1,000,080	1,000,080	1,207,484
26	70	0	90,000	0	−90,000	976,928	976,928	1,123,467
27	71	0	60,000	30,000	−90,000	952,420	952,420	1,080,301
28	72	0	0	90,000	−90,000	925,923	925,923	1,041,682
29	73	0	0	90,000	−90,000	897,253	897,253	998,313
30	74	0	0	90,000	−90,000	866,320	866,320	949,996
Total		600,000	600,000	300,000	−300,000			
31	75	0	0	90,000	−90,000	833,045	833,045	895,540
32	76	0	0	90,000	−90,000	796,793	796,793	864,095
33	77	0	0	90,000	−90,000	757,299	757,299	828,484
34	78	0	0	90,000	−90,000	714,276	714,276	789,418
35	79	0	0	90,000	−90,000	667,426	667,426	746,592
36	80	0	0	90,000	−90,000	616,383	616,383	699,634
37	81	0	0	90,000	−90,000	560,774	560,774	648,184
38	82	0	0	90,000	−90,000	500,197	500,197	591,772
39	83	0	0	90,000	−90,000	434,215	434,215	530,011
40	84	0	0	90,000	−90,000	362,336	362,336	462,378
Total		600,000	600,000	1,200,000	−1,200,000			

Yr.	Age	Premium Outlay $	Partial Withdrawal $	Net Loan $	Annual Net Outlay $	Accum. Value Less Loans $	Cash Surrender Value $	Death Benefit $
41	85	0	0	90,000	-90,000	284,015	284,015	388,315
42	86	0	0	90,000	-90,000	198,703	198,703	307,258
43	87	0	0	90,000	-90,000	105,780	105,780	218,570
44	88	0	0	0	0	101,631	101,631	218,783
45	89	0	0	0	0	96,073	96,073	217,710
46	90	0	0	0	0	88,268	88,268	214,501
47	91	0	0	0	0	80,279	80,279	185,070
48	92	0	0	0	0	72,657	72,657	154,240
49	93	0	0	0	0	66,179	66,179	122,702
50	94	0	0	0	0	61,766	61,766	91,156
Total		600,000	600,000	1,470,000	-1,470,000			
51	95	0	0	0	0	56,370	56,370	86,929
52	96	0	0	0	0	49,874	49,874	81,643
53	97	0	0	0	0	42,146	42,146	75,167
54	98	0	0	0	0	33,044	33,044	67,359
55	99	0	0	0	0	22,410	22,410	58,063
Total		600,000	600,000	1,470,000	-1,470,000			

If he pays $30,000 a year into this policy for 20 years, from age 45 to 65, the cash value could grow to $1,000,000, assuming the policy pays a 6% interest rate. Then at 65, he stops paying into the policy and starts taking out $40,000 a year in tax-free loans. He can do this for 30 years without destroying the policy, or he could take out $60,000 a year, tax-free, for 20 years. He will be able to take out over twice as much as he put in, all tax-free, and still have a death benefit of $700,000 or more. (Note: These figures are approximations—averages of figures from several insurance companies—and are in no way meant to be exact. Call your insurance agent or financial advisor for figures.)

This plan uses all the advantages of sound financial planning. Dave must be careful not to take out *all of the cash value* or the policy could collapse, and then all of the withdrawals made up to then would become *taxable*. This must be avoided and will be if he never takes out more than about 80% of the cash value. The taxes on all these withdrawals 20 years later, plus penalties and interest for 20 years of not paying taxes on the withdrawals, would be disastrous. He must be sure to always have some cash value in the policy or he will have to start paying premiums again to avoid letting the policy collapse.

As you can imagine, there are many different ways to build the cash value inside a life insurance policy and then to use it for tax-free income during retirement. And, of course, if Dave dies before retirement or only a few years into his retirement, the death benefit will be paid out to his estate. He (or his estate) wins either way.

Estate Taxes

The other general exception to the rule that you only buy life insurance to protect your financial dependents—those who are dependent on your income—is when the insurance is used to pay your estate taxes. Paying your estate taxes is a way of protecting your dependents, or heirs, as it keeps your estate intact so the family's long-range plans can be achieved. This applies only to large estates—generally over $2,000,000—where there will be a lot of taxes to pay. Properly set up, the insurance can pay the taxes so that the heirs get the entire estate. The first $675,000 of each person's estate is normally tax-free because of the personal exemption in the tax law (see table 14.3). The $675,000 exemption can be doubled to $1,350,000 in the case of a husband and wife *if* they set up a proper living trust to hold their estate. So estate taxes become a problem only in the case of a single person with an estate much larger than $675,000, say $1,000,000 or more, or a married couple with an estate much larger than $1,350,000, say $2,000,000 or more. There are obviously many variations to these large estates and the way to provide for them.

Table 14.3   Estate and Gift Tax Exclusion

		Exclusion
Through	1998	$600,000
	1999	650,000
	2000	675,000
	2001	675,000
	2002	700,000
	2003	700,000
	2004	850,000
	2005	950,000
	2006	1,000,000

To pay estate taxes, a single person will want a low-cost, low-cash-value universal life policy that he or she can pay up in 10 to 20 years or pay with a single payment. A married couple should get a low-cost survivor life policy. This is an interesting type of policy that pays only when the second spouse dies, which is when the taxes, if any, are due. No estate taxes are due when the first spouse dies, when the estate is passed between spouses. Therefore, no life insurance proceeds are needed when the first spouse dies. Normally, insuring two people requires two life insurance policies, but with survivor life, only one policy is required, which reduces the cost of insurance by 30% to 40%. This policy can also be bought with a single payment if desired, which is often the least expensive way.

You are going to be rich, with $2,000,000 in liquid assets, so this applies to you. Your estate could owe a lot of taxes! That's good because it means you've achieved your goals. Be prepared.

Life insurance can also be used in a few other very special situations such as to provide charitable gifts or to create an additional estate at your death in case you have not built an adequate estate during your lifetime. However, the basic uses of life insurance are for family protection, additional retirement income, or payment of estate taxes.

As your estate grows and your need for retirement income increases, you will need to find a qualified financial advisor to help you plan your life insurance. Generally, you will need only one policy on any person, plus a survivor policy if needed to pay estate taxes. Be sure to shop around. Prices can vary as much as 100% from company to company.

Rather than having two individual life policies, it is usually better to have one larger policy. For example, you have a 10-year-old policy for $100,000 and you decide you need $200,000 of coverage. Check the cost of a single $200,000 policy, rather than adding another $100,000 policy to your existing coverage. In this case, a $250,000 policy might be even better, as there is often a price break at $250,000. A good advisor can help a lot as your needs increase.

Don't be oversold on life insurance. Some insurance agents are very persuasive. Remember that your plan is to grow rich, and life insurance costs money and is only one step in a seven-step process. It is not the whole process. The premiums must be paid for out of the 10% (or more) of your income you are using in your plan to get rich.

At the same time, don't be underinsured, either. A properly selected cash value life insurance policy offers many benefits during your lifetime. Take advantage of them while you are protecting your family.

Chapter 15
Picking Your Investments: Steps 3 and 4

Right now, over 11,000 mutual funds are available in the United States. In addition, thousands of individual stocks are listed on the New York, American, and NASDAQ stock exchanges. Then there are bonds—corporate, treasury, and municipal bonds—plus stock options, various bond derivatives, real-estate investment trusts (REITs), convertible bonds, preferred stock, and all sorts of limited partnerships. These are all available to you, the investor, to meet your investment needs. You now know that a simple savings account or CD is not enough to help you get rich—you have to look at other investments. You are the boss, you have the money, you have a goal, and you must choose. But how do you choose wisely those investments that will help you grow rich?

Ask a Friend

One way to begin is to talk to friends who are successful investors. (Be sure they are truly successful and not just big talkers.) Ask how they do it, what funds or other investments they use, who their advisors or brokers are, and what they recommend. Then start checking. Check funds in the *Morningstar Reports* and send for information. Meet your friends' brokers and ask for references. This is critical. Don't just take someone's word for it regarding investment advice. It's your money you're investing so be careful. Remember, you are looking for an average annual return of 12% or better.

Financial Planners

A second way to begin is to look for, and interview, good financial planners. The Financial Planners Association (FPA) can send you the names of certified financial planners in your area. Call FPA at (800) 322-4237, extension 2, or visit www.fpanet.org on the Internet. CFPs will help you with all aspects of your plan: cash flow, cash reserves, insurance needs, investments, retirement plans, taxes and tax planning, and estate plans and living trusts to protect your family. Again, investigate these certified financial planners carefully and get references. If you are not satisfied with what you find, keep looking. Very good planners/advisors are available in all parts of the country. So are some bad ones. Find out what training a planner has had and whether he or she is a "fee only" or "commissions only" advisor or whether the planner earns commissions/fees from the investments and advice he or she provides. The way a planner is compensated may (or may not) have a bearing on what the advisor recommends.

If you choose a planner or broker to help you, he or she will make recommendations on various investments. Check out those recommendations. Ask your planner to show you the investment's past performance over 5 or 10 years. Ask why your planner thinks that investment is right for you. If you agree, go ahead and invest. If it sounds too good to be true, as the old adage says, it probably is.

If you work with an advisor or broker for a few years and your results are not good enough to meet your goal, start looking again. Remember, it's your money and you must make whatever choices are necessary to reach your goal.

Also remember that you are developing a long-range plan, so you want to look at long-range investments. Unless you are going to be a very active trader and fund-switcher (timer), you want to buy long-range investments. You will need to make changes from time to time but not frequently. You will want to understand long-range trends over the last 10 and 20 years. What is the long-range trend of interest rates? Are they going up or down? What about gross domestic product (GDP) and experts? (Note: gross domestic product is the total value of all the goods and services produced in this country in one year. It is currently about $7.25 trillion.) What about inflation? Is it increasing? What industries are leading our economy? You don't need to be an expert, but it is good to be aware of the economic trends and to have a basic understanding of them and their impact on your money. If you are not interested in these economic matters, then be sure your advisor keeps up with them.

Mutual Funds

By far the easiest and most common way to invest is through mutual funds. If you are just starting or have no special knowledge of investing, then start with mutual funds. Picking stocks is both an art and a science that few people have natural ability in. Mutual funds hire managers for growth funds because of their skill in picking stocks. These skilled managers then work for you every day while you are concentrating your skills on your own job.

You can get started in choosing and investing in mutual funds in several ways. The first is to go to your local library and ask the people at the reference desk where you can find by far the most valuable resource: the *Morningstar Reports*. This massive book lists thousands of mutual funds broken down by categories and tells you on one page everything you would want to know about any fund. Morningstar provides information about each fund's historical and current performance, the nature of its investments, and strategy. There are charts and graphs, sales and earnings history, and forecasts. Morningstar even has the toll-free phone number of each fund so you can call for more information about it—literature, a prospectus, and an application. If you like studying investments for yourself, Morningstar is the ideal way to get started.

The library also has scores of books on various aspects of investing: types of investments, real estate, how to invest, successful investors, and on and on. Some are interesting, some are entertaining, and some are boring. For detailed information about specific types of investments, insurance, qualified retirement plans, or other items, look for a thick encyclopedia-type book. The books by or about celebrities don't help much.

Almost all pension plans and corporate retirement plans use mutual funds now, and you should, too. Whether you're investing in an IRA or your personal account, mutual funds are ideal. They have many advantages. You can open an account at most mutual funds for $1,000—at some for as little as $250. They have full-time experts who manage the investments every day. Each fund generally has 100 or more broadly diversified stocks or bonds. The many classes of investment funds, with a broad selection of funds within each class, provide funds for virtually every investor. Some of these classes are

- Aggressive growth funds—fastest increase in sales and profits
- Growth funds—steady in sales and profit over many years
- Growth and income funds—growth stocks that pay large dividends
- Value funds—stocks that are underpriced compared to the market
- Large-cap or blue-chip funds—stocks valued at over $10 billion
- Mid-cap funds—stocks capitalized (valued) at $1 to $10 billion
- Small-cap funds—stocks capitalized (valued) at less than $1 billion
- Tax-managed funds—managed for growth and little or no taxable income each year
- International funds (which exclude U.S. stocks)
- Global funds (which include U.S. stocks)
- European, Pacific, and Latin American funds
- Country funds, such as from Germany, Spain, China, and Japan
- Specialty or sector funds, such as for technology, medical services, biotechnology, telecommunications, precious metals, leisure, energy, and utilities.

Begin with one fund. Select a solid fund with the performance and risk ratings you need. Stay away from funds less than three years old. When you have $5,000 in your chosen fund, you may want to divide it into two or three different types of funds and divide your regular monthly investment into these two or three funds. This diversification greatly reduces your risk without hurting your long-term rate of return. When you have invested up to $20,000 or so, you could start three more funds or stay with one good one. Either way, check your results regularly and make any necessary changes.

In the examples in chapter 1 and the illustrations in chapter 8, I used only mutual funds. That was partly for convenience but mostly because they are the one common, well-known investment that can do the job for you. They are perfect in an IRA and very common in pension plans, profit-sharing plans, 401(k) plans, and other qualified retirement plans.

Variable Annuities

For personal investments that are nonqualified (that is, not in a qualified retirement plan, a plan that qualifies per IRS rules for tax-deductible contributions and tax-deferred earnings), use a variable annuity. This is a combination of several mutual funds (variable) inside a tax-deferred account called an annuity at an insurance company. The variable annuity is also tax-deferred, and its overall earnings are those of the individual funds in it. Every major mutual fund company manages funds in variable annuities, and every major life insurance company offers one or more of them.

A variable annuity is a combination of several mutual funds managed by one or more investment companies and an annuity managed by an insurance company; it is a group of mutual funds wrapped in an annuity. This gives you the choice, selection, and potential high return of mutual funds and the tax deferral of an annuity. Most variable annuities now offer 10 or more investment choices. Just like the funds themselves, these variable annuities offer growth funds, aggressive growth funds, global funds, government bond funds, high-yield bond funds, high-tech funds, natural resource funds, and many others, as well as money market funds and, usually, a fixed interest account. The latter is fully guaranteed by the life insurance company, just like a fixed annuity.

Most variable annuities allow 10 or more exchanges among the various accounts every year. The initial investment required runs a little higher than for mutual funds, usually $1,500 and up. Because two companies are involved, the mutual fund or investment advisor and the life insurance company, the annual fees are about 1%

more than those of a mutual fund. Fees run from 1.0% to 2.5% a year, and hence the rate of return is reduced by about 1%, compared to a similar mutual fund. This, however, is more than compensated for by the fact that the earnings are tax-deferred.

Fixed Annuities

For tax deferral on a guaranteed, fixed-rate investment, use a fixed annuity, often called a single-premium deferred annuity (SPDA). There are many of them; most major life insurance companies offer them. Fixed annuities don't pay anything near the 12% average return you need to become rich, but they do have four big benefits:

1. Annuities are tax-deferred.
2. They are guaranteed by the insurance company.
3. They usually pay you 1% to 2% more than banks pay on CDs.
4. They can be converted into a lifetime income at any time.
    This is called "annuitizing," and it will give you an income you can't outlive.

Based on the money in your annuity and your life expectancy, the insuring company will calculate an income and pay you for life, no matter how long you live. It may be a small amount or a large amount, depending upon how much your account is worth, but it will be for your lifetime. This lifetime income is all of the interest your annuity earns plus a little of the principal in each payment. This way, you get a higher payment every month than just the interest alone. Part of each payment is interest (taxable), and part is return of principal (tax-free). The trade-off is that the issuing company keeps your principal after you die.

You can take an alternative approach to annuities: You don't have to annuitize your annuity. You can treat it just like a bank savings account and put money in and take it out whenever you want. If you choose to do this, you must be aware of three extra rules:

1. Almost all annuities have a surrender charge if you withdraw money in the first 5 to 10 years. Then this charge disappears.
2. When money is taken out, the IRS rule is that the interest comes out first, and the interest is all taxable when withdrawn. So all withdrawals, until you get down to your principal, are taxable. When you withdraw the principal, it is tax-free because it was "after-tax" money when you put it in the annuity.
3. If you take money out of your annuity before age 59-$\frac{1}{2}$, there is an additional 10% federal tax penalty. Many states also have an early withdrawal penalty.

So use your annuity for retirement. That's what it's designed for. But remember the four big advantages: tax deferral, guaranteed returns, higher fixed interest, and the possibility of lifetime income.

Of the many other kinds of investments, these three—mutual funds, variable annuities, and fixed annuities—are the most dependable. Options and other derivatives are at least 10 times more risky. Options have a time limit, usually about three to six months, and you can lose all of your money in them—100%! Trading futures is even more risky, as you can actually lose 100% of your investment and still owe the broker money. That's no way to get rich.

Stocks and bonds also introduce a higher level of risk in many cases. Good government bonds are certainly safe, but in times of high inflation, 4% or more, you rapidly lose your purchasing power by holding bonds.

Stocks are volatile, and even IBM, General Motors, Microsoft, AOL, and Texaco stock can drop by 20%, 30%, or more in a short time. If that drop happens to occur about the time you are planning to retire, you could lose a lot of your retirement money. Of course, stocks go up, too. You don't have to sell them just because they go down. They might bounce right back, or they might come back slowly over time. Historically, stocks have proven themselves to be the best investment. The question is, How much time do you have?

A good advisor is important because there are no guaranteed 12% accounts. That kind of return requires effort on your part or on the part of a good advisor.

You must keep your eye on your goal and check where you are every year. Compare your position to a 12% rate of return. Are you ahead of your projections or behind? Discuss the situation with your advisor and make whatever adjustments you have to. If you're right on course, then just keep going. The goal is $2,000,000, a splendid retirement and a legacy of wealth for your family, starting with you.

Chapter 16
Using the Tax Laws: Step 5

Planning your income and expenses can make a big difference in how much you owe in taxes each year. Starting with your current income, as in Form 1—Income, begin to think about changes you can make in the future to reduce your taxable income or to convert taxable to tax-free income.

Deductions

You may be able to increase your deductions and thus reduce your taxes this year. How? First look at the general categories of deductions and study them. Spend enough time each year (it will take only an hour or two) to see what deductions apply to you and determine how you can use them to your advantage.

The total of all the deductions you list on Schedule A of your federal tax form must *exceed* your standard deduction, which is determined by the government, or you haven't gained anything. You can claim either your list of deductions or your standard deduction, whichever is greater. You can't have both.

The standard deductions in 2000 are

Single person	$4,400
Head of household	6,450
Married filing jointly	7,350
Married filing separately	3,675

Let's look at some of these and see how you can take advantage of them. Keep track of every dime in deductions. Also study the list and see how you can rearrange your expenses next year so that some of your regular costs (e.g., for clothing, commuting, subscriptions, or classes) can be claimed as deductions.

Many of these deductions are based on a percentage of your adjusted gross income (AGI), which is line 31 on form 1040 or line 16 on form 1040A.

Charitable Contributions

At least once a year, go through your closets, pull out your unwanted clothes, and donate them to charity. Get a receipt for them; the charity will gladly give you one.

.nd accurate record of monetary gifts to churches, temples, charities, and
r gift is over $200, you must get a receipt. Look for other items you can
;, a sofa, a lawnmower, golf clubs. Charities will take them all and give
s for everything.

If you sponsor or strongly support a nonprofit or charitable organization, plan your giving in a way that will most benefit your own tax and income needs. For example, give more or less each year depending on your income and other factors. Keep track of the miles driven while doing charity work, going to and from the charity, for example, because those miles are a deductible expense, figured at 14 cents per mile. For charitable deductions, there is generally a maximum you can claim in any one year of 50% of your AGI.

Other Deductions

Medical expenses must exceed 7.5% of your AGI before you can deduct them. These expenses can include those for doctors, chiropractors, some other health practitioners, hospitals, prescription drugs, and other medicines, even the fee for parking your car at the doctor's office or the hospital. Keep accurate records for yourself and all of your dependents.

Casualty and theft losses in excess of 10% of your AGI can be deducted. These losses must be nonreimbursed, and there is a $100 deductible for each item and for each person.

Job expenses, too, can be substantial each year. Look at the list at the end of this section and see how big a deduction you can build. These expenses must exceed 2% of your AGI before you can claim them.

Investment expenses—that is, the cost of looking after your investments—are deductible when they exceed 2% of your AGI.

Did you know that the fee you pay your tax preparer is deductible as an investment expense? Also, any cost you have in maintaining your investments, such as management fees, a subscription to the *Wall Street Journal* or other publications or investment letters, a safe deposit box, interest on money borrowed to invest, and many more such items are deductible.

Interest paid on your primary residence and on your second home is fully deductible.

State and local taxes are generally deductible in full, without any "floor" or minimum level, such as 2% of your AGI, to exceed. This deduction includes all state and local (and foreign) income taxes in the year you pay them and also all state and local real property taxes and personal property taxes.

If you own a business, you can save additional taxes by claiming depreciation. This is a wonderful accounting device that allows you to take a deduction from income each year equal to the dollar amount any given piece of equipment, including automobiles, computers, and software, has depreciated that year.

Even if you don't own a business but use your car on your job, you can claim some depreciation for it. That's another expense that reduces the taxes you pay.

Hundreds of other items can be added to your list of deductions. Some of the most common ones are listed below. Be sure to check each item in the IRS rules for its deductibility or with your CPA before you claim it. Not all are 100% deductible.

Airfares	Labor union dues
Auto club membership	Laundry
Auto expenses	Legal expenses
Books used on the job	Local transportation
Business machines	Lodging
Car insurance premiums	Magazines
Christmas gifts	Malpractice liability premiums
Cleaning costs	Meals
Commerce association dues	Medical examinations
Commuting costs	Membership dues and fees
Computers	Motel charges
Convention trips	Moving expenses
Copying costs	Parking fees
Correspondence courses	Passport fees for business travel
Depreciation	Pay turned over to employer
Dues	Periodicals
Educational expenses	Protective clothing
Employment agency fees	Rail fares
Entertainment expenses	Reimbursed expenses
Equipment	Safety shoes
Fax charges	Secretarial expenses
Fidelity bond costs	Subscriptions
Foreign travel cost	Taxi fares
Furniture	Telegrams
Garage rent	Telephone calls
Gasoline	Toll charges
Gasoline taxes	Tools
Gifts	Trade association dues
Helmets	Transportation travel expenses
Home office expenses	Tuition
Hotel costs	Uniforms
House-hunting costs	Union dues
Instruments	Work clothes and uniforms

After you subtract all your losses, your contributions, and your deductions, then you figure your taxes.

Review all of this with your tax preparer so you can build large deductions for yourself. You could also buy an annual tax guide. Many guides are available in bookstores and cost about $15.

Tax Credits

Are deductions the end of the possibilities? Not at all. Now you can take any tax credits you may have. These are for expenses for care of children or dependents, care for elderly dependents, foreign tax credits, and others. "Others" includes low-income-housing credits.

You may not be aware of it, but you can actually purchase tax credits by investing in low-income housing. Low-income-housing investment partnerships are available to the general public for as little as $5,000. The partnerships buy and/or build low-income housing primarily for the elderly in rural areas. These programs are strictly supervised by the U.S. government and provide needed housing mostly for retired people trying to get by on Social Security or other low income.

You, the investor, usually receive about 110% of your investment back in tax credits over a 10-year period, plus your share of the value of the property when it is sold. On a $10,000 investment, the investor should get approximately $1,100 a year in tax credits each year for 10 years. Then the property would be sold and the investor would get back a proportionate share of the property's worth.

This is a sophisticated tax and investment strategy, but it can be very valuable. Many wealthy investors and major corporations invest in low-income-housing partnerships each year as a very sure way to reduce their taxes. So can you.

As I've mentioned many times, reducing your taxes each year saves you money, which you can either spend or invest.

If you get a tax refund of more than $300 to $400, you need to refigure your tax withholding or quarterly payments. Don't lend the IRS more than its fair share of your money. You should keep your money and invest it.

So far, we have looked only at federal income taxes. Most states also have income tax structures. Only six states have none: Alaska, Florida, Nevada, South Dakota, Washington, and Wyoming. In fact, many people move to those states when they retire just to avoid state taxes.

Tax-Free Income

You can't talk about taxes and making the right choices without mentioning municipal bonds, tax-free bond funds, tax-deferred annuities, and the cash value of a life insurance policy. Each has a specific and useful role in your rise to riches.

There is a place in everyone's portfolio for safe, guaranteed investments. That is the place for tax-free municipal bonds and municipal bond funds and tax-deferred annuities. Triple A rated municipal bonds are as safe as U.S. government bonds, and they are tax-free. That makes them a better, more useful investment than a taxable bond with the same interest rate. For investors who own bond funds for their income, a tax-free bond income fund makes more sense than a taxable bond income fund of the same quality. A California tax-free bond fund is free of California state taxes and also free of federal taxes. Tax-free municipal bonds and bond funds are available in almost every state, and they are state and federal tax-free.

The more taxable income you have, the higher your tax rate becomes, the more taxes you pay, and the more money you give away. A wealthy widow I know is worth millions. She has some long-term growth variable annuities to keep up with inflation, and her income investments are all in municipal bond funds. Last year, her taxable income was just under $6,000. All the rest of her income is tax-free! She uses the tax laws very well and lives very well.

Annuities are not only tax-deferred (that is, you pay no taxes on the earnings of your savings while they are accumulating), they are also guaranteed by the insurance company that issues them. That means you have a guaranteed, tax-deferred, high-interest savings account when you own an annuity. Besides being guaranteed and tax-deferred, annuities often pay 1% to 2% more interest than bank savings accounts. Given the choice, what would you want? Lower interest and taxable income or higher interest and tax-deferred income?

For extra-safe long-term savings, use annuities. For long-term regular income, use tax-free municipal bond funds. For shorter-term accounts, when you may need to use some of the money from time to time, use short-to-intermediate-term tax-free municipal bond funds. Some of these funds even allow check writing!

Life Insurance Cash Value

The cash value inside a life insurance policy accumulates tax-free. In chapter 1, we mentioned Dr. Dave, 45, who was starting to rebuild his financial world after his divorce. One part of his plan was a high-cash-value life insurance policy that cost him $30,000 a year. What was his plan and why was the insurance so expensive?

There were three parts to his plan:

1. To provide adequate life insurance and death benefits to his heirs
2. To accumulate money tax-free
3. To provide tax-free income for himself during his retirement

We examined the insurance aspects of his decision in detail in chapter 14. Now we'll discuss the tax benefits.

Accumulating money tax-free, of course, is a much more effective strategy for building wealth than paying taxes on your investment earnings every year. The cash value buildup inside a life insurance policy is tax-free by law. So if you need life insurance, and Dr. Dave does, this tax-free buildup is a big benefit.

In fact, Dave selected a policy with the maximum cash value buildup. He chose the maximum because of another tax benefit: When he retires, he can borrow tax-free against this cash value. This will be a major part of his retirement income.

The process works like this: Dave puts as much cash as possible into his life insurance policy while he is working, in his case $30,000 a year. This will give him a cash value within the insurance policy of between $550,000 and $750,000 when he retires at age 60, depending on the insurance company and current interest rates. He can then borrow against this cash value, using *interest-free loans* as provided for in the policy. He should be able to take out loans and withdrawals of $40,000 per year for 20 years or more. If he continues to work and puts the maximum amount into his policy to age 65, he could take out $60,000 a year for 20 years or more. The loan is allowed to accumulate during Dave's lifetime and is paid back out of the policy proceeds at Dave's death. (This strategy is quite common and is explained in full detail in chapter 14.)

His loans and withdrawals are tax-free income. Loans, of course, are always tax-free (but not interest free) whether they are loans from an insurance policy or bank loans to buy a new car. And withdrawals of principal from the policy are also tax-free. Remember, Dave paid in $30,000 a year for 15 years, a total of $450,000. But that money compounds over the years. If he takes out $40,000 a year for 20 years, that is $800,000 he takes out—much more than he paid in—all tax-free!

By choosing to use the tax laws to his advantage, Dave is maximizing the cash value in his life insurance policy by putting in the most allowed, then he will use that cash value to provide himself with a guaranteed tax-free income of $40,000 to $60,000 per year for 20 years or more—and he still will have the life insurance. By taking out less money per year, he can have income for more years, even up to age 100 and beyond.

Building cash value is a complicated procedure. If you are interested, get several proposals from a knowledgeable financial advisor or several life insurance companies.

At every stage of the process of accumulating wealth, you have choices that involve the tax laws. You can either invest with tax-deductible dollars or after-tax dollars. You can accumulate with taxable or tax-deferred earnings or taxable or tax-free interest. And finally, you can withdraw your money during retirement as taxable income or tax-free income or tax-free loans.

At every step, make the choices that will be of the most benefit to you.

Study Your Income

Go back to Form 1—Income, which you filled out in chapter 2. Taxes are probably your biggest single expense, so you want to consciously and deliberately build up tax-free or tax-deferred income. Therefore, as a start, put an *x* (indicating a tax benefit) in front of each item of income that is tax-deferred or tax-free.

For example:

- Dividends paid on a mutual fund *in your IRA* are tax-deferred—*x*
- Interest earned in an annuity is tax-deferred—*x*
- Interest earned on municipal bonds is tax-free—*x*
- Life insurance interest is tax-free—*x*

This shows you whether you are using the tax laws or not. It also makes you look at *all* the income you are earning. If you understand all of your income, then you can work on all of it. Keep moving your money to get higher returns and tax-free returns.

Study Your Assets

Now look at Form 2—Assets, which you also completed in chapter 2 and do the same exercise. Study each item on the list, and if there is a tax benefit in it, put an *x* in front of it.

For example:

- Interest on your home's mortgage is tax-deductible—*x*
- Interest on the mortgage on a second home, yacht, or motorhome is tax-deductible—*x*
- The cost of medical devices is a medical expense and can be a deduction—*x*
- If you use your car for business, you can deduct a mileage factor—*x*
- Income property is a separate business and generates lots of deductions—*x*
- Investments can have tax benefits, as mentioned in the discussion of Form 1 above.

Study Form 2 again and see if it suits your plan for riches. Separate in your mind the possessions you own just because you enjoy them—artwork, antiques, expensive cars, golf clubs—from the possessions you own because they will help you to become rich.

Be completely aware of how much the possessions you own for pleasure cost each year for maintenance and how much you spend each year for more of these items. Then be aware of how much your investments cost each year and how much you invest in building your assets each year. You must know these facts intimately so that you can make the right choices as you go along. You need both pleasure and investments. You are working for both.

Finally, check the tax benefits of your income and your assets every year. The first week of January is a good time for this.

Your money is being spent on taxes. Spend as little as you can and use your tax savings to build your riches.

Chapter 17
You're Rich!

You've done it. You're rich! Or at least you know how to become rich and are well on your way to riches. Ben Franklin said, "Well begun is half done." If you have a new attitude that says, "I am becoming wealthy, I am becoming rich," and if you have made new choices about the way you will handle your money and the way you look at yourself and your finances, then you are, indeed, well begun and half done.

The next question is, What do you do with your accumulated wealth? A first thought that comes to many people is "spend it." You have spent half a lifetime, maybe more, to become rich and now you have $2,000,000. Is that what you want to do, spend it?

Do you build a house—brick by brick, board by board—then when it is finished just tear it down? Demolish it? Destroy it?

Enjoy It

To build a wonderful house takes time and effort and lots of sweat. When completed, it's just what you wanted. You have dreamed about having a house and your desire was the force that pushed you along until it was done. Why would you destroy it?

And why would you spend your $2,000,000? You have built it carefully over time. Your desire has pushed you forward and carried you through some tough times to get where you are now. You have made a lot of right choices. You are a different person from the one who began this journey years ago.

Your $2,000,000 is a part of you. If you built a house you would move in, live in it, take care of it, and enjoy it. You might even hope your children would use it and enjoy it, too.

The same is true of your wealth. Live with it, enjoy it, use it, and take care of it. You built it; now get the benefit of it.

Taken care of properly, your wealth will last forever—literally. That was part of the original plan, and you have succeeded so far.

Taking care of your wealth is not easy, but by this time you will have a pretty good idea of how to go about it. You have built up this pile of money, these investments, and you want it to last. You want it to last through your lifetime, and you'd like your children to enjoy the benefits of what you have built.

And, of course, it has to support you in your retirement. No more hard work. No more drudgery. No more time clocks. And no more paychecks.

From Growth to Income

Let's assume you've reached your goal. Now your money must be invested to generate income. Up until now, you have been interested only in growth—maximum growth of 12% to 20% a year or more. You weren't concerned about dividends or interest rates or cash flow. You wanted growth, long-term capital gains, and the bigger the better.

Now you can retire and let your money generate the income you need. This is not quite as simple as it sounds, but it is not difficult, either. It just has to be done carefully, thoughtfully. You don't want to pay a lot of extra taxes, and you don't want to take chances.

First, ask yourself how much income you need from your money. If you were earning $40,000 a year before you retired, then you will probably need about $40,000 a year now. A little more or less is fine. One expense you won't have is investing into your retirement plan; therefore, you may need a little less. If you earned $70,000 a year when you were working, then you will probably need about $70,000 now. If you earned $120,000, then you need about $120,000 now. That's a start. Many Americans believe the myth that you won't need as much income when you retire. However, most people need just about the same amount to maintain their comfortable lifestyle. Few people change their lifestyle in retirement.

Your Retirement Income

The income you need in retirement can be earned in a variety of ways. For example:
- $40,000 a year is $2,000,000 earning 2% ($2,000,000 \times 0.02 = 40,000$), or $40,000 is $666,000 earning 6% in safe U.S. Treasury bonds with the remaining $1,334,000 still invested.
- $70,000 a year is $2,000,000 earning 3.5% ($2,000,000 \times 0.35 = 70,000$) or $1,166,000 earning 6% with the remaining $833,000 still invested.
- $120,000 a year is $2,000,000 earning 6%.

Typically, U.S. Treasury bonds, the safest investment, will earn about 4.5–6% or more. It is easy to turn your money into a guaranteed income stream by buying treasury bonds. However, treasury bonds may not be the best choice for you. You may want more than just an income, or you may want tax-free income instead of taxable income. You want your wealth to continue to grow at least as fast as inflation, and you want to keep taxes low. You may also want to use some of your wealth to fulfill a long-held dream: a new house, a cabin somewhere, a retirement home, travel, donations to charity, educational or spiritual endeavors, or some other dream.

Therefore, converting some or all of your growth investments that built your wealth into income-generating investments may not be so simple. Two areas are of concern in converting your growth investments to income investments:

1. The determination of how much of your investments to allocate to income. How much should go into ultrasafe treasury bonds? How much into higher-yielding bonds or tax-free bonds, leaving more money for growth investments and other needs? If you take out $250,000 for a special project, then how do you change the remaining investments so they will generate the same income?

2. The tax consequences of this conversion. Taxes at this stage of your life, and with this amount of money, can be huge and devastating. Taxes can run from 10% to 50% of the sum of money you move from one investment to another, and the income generated from the investments can be taxable, whereas most of your growth investments were tax-deferred.

When working out your retirement income, first you must know the amount of income you will need and look at the investments you have. How much income are they generating for you now? If it is enough to meet your income needs, then the problem is already solved and you can go right on to the second area of concern. To see what your current income is, fill in Form 4—Retirement Income.

Form 4   Retirement Income

Your total income consists of the following items:

Income Needed
    Gross income, before taxes $ _____
        OR
    Net income, after taxes $ _____

Noninvestment Income
    Social Security $ _____
    Spouse's Social Security   _____
    Pension #1   _____
    Pension #2   _____
    Retirement pay   _____
    Other current income:
        Payments you receive
        (loan payments, mortgages, rents, etc.):   _____
    Total income without investments $ _____

Investment Income
    Qualified Plans (IRA, 401(k), 403(b), and other)
        Item #1 _____ $ _____
        Item #2 _____   _____
        Item #3 _____   _____
    Fixed Income (CDs, annuities, insurance cash value, bonds)
        Item #1 _____   _____
        Item #2 _____   _____
        Item #3 _____   _____
        Item #4 _____   _____
    Growth Investments (stocks, growth funds, variable annuities)
        Item #1 _____   _____
        Item #2 _____   _____
        Item #3 _____   _____
        Item #4 _____   _____
    Total investment income $ _____

Income Needed

List the estimated gross income you need and include income to pay your income taxes; if your income is mostly tax-free (from tax-free bonds), then just list your net after-tax income. You can estimate your taxes at 20% or at 25% if you have high state taxes. If your income will be over $100,000 per year, then figure your tax rate at 30% or 35%.

Outside Income

Next, write down what you'll receive from Social Security and what your spouse will receive. Then list other pensions and retirement plans that you and your spouse may be entitled to. Some people may collect as many as three full pensions. Finally, add in any other miscellaneous income you have, such as interest from outstanding loans or mortgages, businesses you own, consultant fees, director's fees, and so on. Also include income from rental property and payments you receive for an asset you sold. Add up these items and see how close the total comes to the income you need.

Note that this income is all *outside of* and *separate from* your investments. Most people have considerable retirement income that is not dependent on their investments.

If the income in the table meets your income needs, your problem is solved, or at least this is one solution. There could be many, many more. In this case, you can maintain your growth-oriented investment portfolio, and it will continue to grow as it has in the past. You might, however, want to take a more conservative approach to your investing now, even if you don't need income, or a lot of income, from your investments. Now that you have reached your goal, there is no sense in taking any more risk than necessary. In this case, reduce the risk by moving from aggressive growth funds to growth funds, then to growth and income funds, then to balanced funds, and then perhaps to some bond funds.

If some of your investments are tax-deferred, such as an IRA or an annuity, it is an easy matter—and fully legal—to start taking the income from these investments. Just write to the investment or insurance company, saying you are retiring and want to take a regular income, and the company will gladly arrange it for you. There are no penalties, either for tax or early withdrawal, if you are taking the interest earned on a long-term basis for your retirement.

You need to be careful of two pitfalls when withdrawing money from these:

1. If the money is from an annuity, you probably should not annuitize. Take the interest, and make it very clear to the insurance company that you are *not* annuitizing. To annuitize means to sign over your hard-earned principal to the

nsurance company. It will then be out of your estate. It will not go to your beneficiaries; it will go to the insurance company, which will keep the principal on your death, in exchange for giving you a lifetime income. Sometimes annu-itizing is the right choice, but many times it is not. It seems to work best for elderly individuals, sometimes those with health problems who are very con-cerned about having enough income or outliving their income. They are usually living alone.

2. If the money is in an IRA and *if you are less than 59-1/2*, arrange to take the money out in *substantially equal monthly payments* until you are 59-1/2 or for five years, whichever is longer. If you withdraw money in any other way before age 59-1/2, you will incur a 10% federal tax penalty on these withdrawals, in addition to the regular income tax, plus state tax penalties in most states. Setting up substantially equal payments for five years or to age 59-1/2 avoids this penalty (IRS Rule 72J).

The money coming out of your annuities or IRAs will be taxed as ordinary income, just as if you were working and getting a paycheck. There is no additional penalty for withdrawing your money. If you work and earn $40,000, you owe tax on $40,000. If you are retired and take $40,000 out of an IRA, you owe tax on it. It's the same tax exactly.

If the total income in Form 4 is less than you need, you can provide additional cur-rent income for yourself by switching from high-growth investments to a safer mixture of mostly income and some growth investments. In general, bonds and mort-gages pay fixed rates of return (called "interest") for income, and stocks pay little or no current income (called "dividends") because they are investments for ownership and are designed for growth. So in retirement, for safety of principal, you can move from growth to income, from stocks to bonds. Obviously, you want to invest in the highest paying and safest income investments you can find. Ranked according to safety, income investments look like this:

1. U.S. Treasury bills, notes, and bonds (T-bills, T-bonds)
2. U.S. government agency certificates: GNMA, FNMA (Federal National Mortgage Association, "Fannie Mae"), FMAC (Franchise Mortgage Acceptance Company)
3. High-grade corporate bonds (AAA, AA, A, BBB)
4. Lower-grade corporate bonds (BB, B, C, unrated)
5. Foreign government and corporate bonds

As the quality of an investment descends, because of the added risk associated with it, the interest rates paid to the investor rise. Therefore, you may want some high-yield bond funds as part of your portfolio. Since this income stream from your investments is the most important asset you will have for the rest of your life, you should develop your portfolio with the help of your financial advisor.

Remember inflation? It's still a factor, and your income must increase regularly to keep pace. In addition to income, you still need growth in your retirement portfolio. To ensure growth, you must maintain growth investments in your portfolio so that the overall value of your portfolio keeps increasing. Twenty years ago, $1,000,000 would have been sufficient to retire on. Now, $2,000,000 is better. At least 10% of your portfolio should always be invested for growth—and 25% would be better.

Tax Considerations

When figuring out your retirement income, be concerned about taxes. Consult with your financial advisor or accountant.

Two major issues should be considered. First, *all* income is taxable unless specifically exempted in the tax law. Congress established that in 1913. So when you start taking income out of your investments, those withdrawals are taxable. When you retire, you automatically receive any pensions or retirement income you are entitled to. You get this whether you want it or not, and it is taxable. If you receive mortgage payments or interest on notes, these are also taxable income to you. If you have rental income or consulting income or other earned income, this is also taxable and part of your tax base.

If you have a very large IRA, you may want to start taking money out of it immediately when you retire rather than letting it accumulate in your estate, where it could be subject to large tax penalties upon your death.

A New Point of View

Normally, you should avoid taking money out of IRAs and other plans until you absolutely need to for income reasons or to comply with the minimum distribution rules. After all, money left in an IRA will continue to grow tax-deferred, as it did during your working years. But now that you have money, now that you are rich, you must start thinking about the tax laws from a rich person's point of view and become concerned about conserving your wealth and protecting your family's estate. You built this wealth over many years. Don't let the tax collector get most of it when you die. The rules are different when you are rich. Details that you thought would never be a problem now could be.

One final note here. If you are over 70-$\frac{1}{2}$ and take out less than the required minimum from your IRA or other qualified plan, you are subject to a *50% penalty* tax on the amount *not* distributed. So be sure to take out enough.

Social Security

You are entitled to collect your Social Security (S/S) benefits in retirement. You get the full benefit at age 65. You can collect 80% of *that* starting at 62. Or you can wait up to age 70 when you are required to take it, and your benefit payment will increase by 8% between 65 and 70. Also, after age 65 you can have as much other income as you want without losing any Social Security benefit. Before age 65, Social Security benefits are reduced if you have excess income, as follows:

Age 62–64   Lose $1 of S/S benefit for every $2 earned in excess of $10,080
Age 65–70   No loss of benefits (2000 tax law)

Because of this rule, in many cases it pays to wait to collect your Social Security until age 65, when there is no limit on the amount of earnings you can have.

Annuities

Your annuities are a much simpler matter. They are not an estate problem. The money in your annuities accumulated and grew tax-deferred, and it is taxed as you withdraw it and use it. There is a tax penalty of 10% for early withdrawal before age 59$\frac{1}{2}$, just like an IRA. No penalty applies in the case of death or disability. Also, there is no minimum distribution requirement when you reach age 70$\frac{1}{2}$.

Annuities pass by law to your heirs. No probate is involved. After age 59$\frac{1}{2}$, you can take any amount of money out of an annuity. By law, the interest and other earnings always come out first and are 100% taxable. Then the principal comes out and it is not taxed. This was your money to begin with. In most cases, be careful not to annuitize, as that takes any money left in the annuity at your death out of your estate and gives it to the insurance company, not to your beneficiary. There are a few exceptions (see chapter 15). The guaranteed lifetime income after annuitization gives some people the sense of security they need. Now that you are rich, you can afford to give some of your wealth to charities, but I have yet to meet anyone whose favorite charity is his or her life insurance company.

Here again, have your investment advisors help you set up your annuities so that you are taking out either the interest or other periodic withdrawals without annuitizing them. You can do this with either fixed annuities or variable annuities.

Life Insurance

If you have a variable life, universal life, or whole life insurance policy and are planning to use it for income, have your advisor help you arrange for a steady income stream from the policy. This needs to be done carefully so as not to collapse the policy. The policy will collapse if you withdraw more than about 80% of its cash value. Then you either have to start paying premiums again to keep the policy in force—which most retired people don't want, or can't afford, to do—or the policy lapses, and you will owe taxes on most of the withdrawals you have made. You owe taxes because the cash value grew tax-*deferred* inside the policy. If the policy lapses, all the interest earned inside the policy that has been withdrawn becomes taxable, and the taxes are due immediately. If $100,000 has been borrowed from the cash value, that $100,000 is suddenly taxable income instead of a tax-free loan.

Taking loans from a whole life policy is a tax-free process, as explained in chapter 14, and therefore a most desirable source of income in retirement. Tax-free income is certainly much better than taxable income. If you don't need this income or you need only a portion of what is available in your policy, that's fine. The policy will continue to grow tax-deferred and will be paid out, income tax–free, to your beneficiary.

If you sell a long-term growth investment, like a growth fund, to buy an income investment, like treasury bonds, that is a taxable event and you will owe taxes on the capital gain in your growth investment. This is also true if you transfer your investment inside a family of mutual funds from a growth fund to an income fund. Taxes are due on the gain on all such transfers or sales.

However, if you are using money accumulated inside a variable annuity or variable life insurance policy, then the transfer from the growth account to the income account is *not* taxable. Any transactions inside annuities and life insurance policies are not taxable.

The same is true of IRA accounts, Keogh plans, profit-sharing plans, 401(k) plans, 403(b) plans and all other qualified plans. Transfers between accounts within these plans are not taxable.

In a qualified plan, the taxes start when you begin taking money out of your plan. It was not taxed going into the plan or while it was earning inside the plan, but every dollar coming out of the plan is taxable. All withdrawals from a qualified plan are taxed as ordinary income at your current tax rate. It doesn't matter where the money came from or how much those dollars earned while in your plan. They are all taxed as ordinary income when paid out of your plan.

So, now you are rich and, with just a little final effort, you can set yourself up to be comfortable and happy the rest of your life. In fact, now that your financial concerns are behind you, you will certainly experience a new sense of lightness and freedom.

Chapter 18
Now You Can Retire: Step 6

Do you remember Bill and Pat? They started their get-rich plan when Bill was 30 and their first child was on the way. Bill started putting $250 a month into his company's 401(k) plan and calculated that if they earned an average of 12% in the plan, they would have $1,450,000 in the plan when he was 65.

In actuality, they did better than that. After a few years, Bill increased his monthly contribution to $300, then later to $400, and when the children were through college, he increased the amount to $600. With this, his wife's small IRA, their savings account, their tax-free bond fund, and a variable annuity, they accumulated their $2,000,000 when Bill was 58.

He had traveled a great deal in his job but decided to give it up. Pat had always wanted to travel, too, but hadn't been able to before, so they decided he would retire early and they would travel together about six months out of the year.

This is what their financial picture looked like when they filled out Form 4:

Income Needed	$80,000
Noninvestment Income	
Bill's Social Security (he'll be 62 in 4 years)	0
Pat's Social Security (she'll be 62 in 6 years)	0
Bill's pension	0
Pat's pension	0
Retirement pay	0
Other current income	
(a loan to his brother,	
$300/month, with 2 years	
left to go)	$3,600
Total	$3,600
Investment Income	
Bill's IRA (rolled over from 401(k) plan)	$1,275,000
Pat's IRA (worked for 5.5 years)	93,500
Savings	11,500

Tax-free bond fund	37,000
Variable annuity (includes $66,000 inherited from Pat's mom 7 years ago)	583,000
	$2,000,000

Bill was earning about $80,000 a year when he retired, and Pat had not worked since their youngest child graduated from college. They still had five years to go to pay off their mortgage. (They had never refinanced the home they bought when Bill was 33.)

Bill and Pat looked at their budget in retirement and assumed they would spend a lot less. They figured Bill spent at least $500 a month, $6,000 a year, on his car, clothes, and lunches when he was working—money that they could save now that he was retired. He also would not be putting $7,200 a year into his 401(k) plan, and they didn't need to keep putting $500 a month into their variable annuity. On the other hand, they wanted to travel and knew that would be expensive. As they looked at the numbers more carefully, they decided that they probably couldn't afford to travel for six months each year. Besides, they wanted to spend time in their home and fix it up, as well as have more time with their friends and their children and grandchildren.

So they thought they would try to take two or three long trips each year. They estimated their cost for each trip would be $5,000 to $8,000. This brought their expenses right back to $80,000 a year.

Looking at their assets, they could see that they couldn't earn $80,000 a year without using income from Bill's big IRA rollover. Because Bill was only 58, any money he took out of his IRA would not only be taxable but would incur a 10% IRS penalty for any withdrawals before age 59½. These withdrawals would also be subject to state taxes and penalties. There is an exception to this rule: If you take "substantially equal monthly payments for five years or until age 59½, whichever is longer," the state and federal tax penalties are waived. Therefore, Bill and Pat chose to set up a five-year plan of withdrawals from Bill's IRA.

As they looked at their situation, they realized that they would have to deal with three different time periods in setting up their retirement income. The first period was from age 58 to age 59½, when they had to deal with the 10%+ tax penalty. The second was from age 59½ to age 70, when they could withdraw money from their IRAs and their variable annuity (or not) without penalty. The third period was after age

$70\frac{1}{2}$, when they were required by law to take out specific and increasing amounts from their IRAs to meet IRS rules. This is shown in Table 18.1.

Table 18.1 Tax Consequences of Using Investment Principal and Interest

	Before Age 59.5	Age 59.5 to 70.5	After Age 70.5
Personal Investments			
Mutual funds* Stocks, bonds, CDs	Fully available No tax penalties	Fully available No tax penalties	Fully available No tax penalties
Annuities: fixed rate or variable annuities	All withdrawals are taxed as ordinary income, plus 10% federal penalty for early withdrawal, plus any state penalties**	All withdrawals are taxed as ordinary income; no tax penalties	All withdrawals are taxed as ordinary income; no mandatory distribution requirement
Qualified Investment Plans			
IRAs, 401(k), 403(b) Profit-sharing plans Money purchase Other	All withdrawals are taxed as ordinary income, plus 10% federal penalty for early withdrawal, plus any state penalties**	All withdrawals are taxed as ordinary income; no tax penalties	All withdrawals are taxed as ordinary income; must start regular with-drawals, according to Table 18.2—Minimum IRA Payout

* Surrender charges may be imposed by the investment company on mutual funds, fixed annuities, or variable annuities in the first few years you own them. Check your investments' prospectuses, and ask your advisor.

** There are some exceptions for first home purchases, death or disability, and eligible higher education expenses—tuition, books, fees, supplies, and room and board for yourself, spouse, child, or grandchild. These early withdrawals are 100% taxable but do not carry the extra 10% federal tax penalty plus possible state tax penalties.

Table 18.2 Minimum IRA Payout Starting at Age 70.5

To know how much you must withdraw from your IRA to avoid the 50% penalty, divide the IRA balance by the life expectancy figure shown for your age or the ages of you and your beneficiary. If you have not named a beneficiary for your account, use the figure in the first column of the table. If you have a beneficiary, check the succeeding columns. For example, if you are age 70 at the end of the year and your beneficiary is 65, you would divide your IRA balance by 23.1. For other life expectancies, see IRA Publication 575. *Pension and Annuity Income.*

Age of IRA Owner	No Beneficiary	Age of Beneficiary															
		60	61	62	63	64	65	66	67	68	69	70	71	72	73	74	75
70	16.0	26.2	25.6	24.9	24.3	23.7	23.1	22.5	22.0	21.5	21.1	20.6	20.2	19.8	19.4	19.1	18.8
71	15.3	26.0	25.3	24.7	24.0	23.4	22.8	22.2	21.7	21.2	20.7	20.2	19.8	19.4	19.0	18.6	18.3
72	14.6	25.8	25.1	24.4	23.8	23.1	22.5	21.9	21.3	20.8	20.3	19.8	19.4	18.9	18.5	18.2	17.8
73	13.9	25.6	24.9	24.2	23.5	22.9	22.2	21.6	21.0	20.5	20.2	19.4	19.0	18.5	18.1	17.7	17.3
74	13.2	25.5	24.7	24.0	23.3	22.7	22.0	21.4	20.8	20.2	19.6	19.1	18.6	18.2	17.7	17.3	16.9
75	12.5	25.3	24.6	23.8	23.1	22.4	21.8	21.1	20.5	19.9	19.3	18.8	18.3	17.8	17.3	16.9	16.5
76	11.9	25.2	24.4	23.7	23.0	22.3	21.6	20.9	20.3	19.7	19.1	18.5	18.2	17.5	17.0	16.5	16.1
77	11.2	25.1	24.3	23.6	22.8	22.1	21.4	20.7	20.1	19.4	18.8	18.3	17.7	17.2	16.7	16.2	15.8
78	10.6	25.0	24.2	23.4	22.7	21.9	21.2	20.5	19.9	19.2	18.6	18.0	17.5	16.9	16.4	15.9	15.4
79	10.0	24.9	24.1	23.3	22.6	21.8	21.1	20.4	19.7	19.0	18.4	17.8	17.2	16.7	16.1	15.6	15.1
80	9.5	24.8	24.0	23.2	22.4	21.7	21.0	20.2	19.5	18.9	18.2	17.6	17.0	16.4	15.9	15.4	14.9
81	8.9	24.7	23.9	23.1	22.3	21.6	20.8	20.1	19.4	18.7	18.1	17.4	16.8	16.2	15.7	15.1	14.6
82	8.4	24.6	23.8	23.0	22.3	21.5	20.7	20.0	19.3	18.6	17.9	17.3	16.6	16.0	15.5	14.9	14.4
83	7.9	24.6	23.8	23.0	22.2	21.4	20.6	19.9	19.2	18.5	17.8	17.1	16.5	15.9	15.3	14.7	14.2
84	7.4	24.5	23.7	22.9	22.1	21.3	20.5	19.8	19.1	18.4	17.7	17.0	16.3	15.7	15.1	14.5	14.0
85	6.9	24.5	23.7	22.8	22.0	21.3	20.5	19.7	19.0	18.3	17.6	16.9	16.2	15.6	15.0	14.4	13.8

Sources: IRS Publication 930, IRS Publication 575

Bill and Pat solved the problem of the first time period—the 10%+ penalty for early withdrawal—by setting up a five-year withdrawal plan. They decided to take the full $80,000 a year out of Bill's IRA and not use their other accounts except in emergencies. Their savings of $11,500 and their tax-free bond fund of $37,000 could be drawn on at any time without penalty, so they made nice cash reserves. Bill can take additional money out of their variable annuity without tax penalty in just $1\frac{1}{2}$ years when he reaches age $59\frac{1}{2}$. Pat can withdraw money from her IRA without penalty in $3\frac{1}{2}$ years.

Bill's IRA rollover had $1,275,000 in it, so it would earn an income of $80,000 a year at just 6.3% interest. He figured they wouldn't have too much trouble earning 6.3% a year, so his IRA wouldn't ever be depleted. They also had sufficient money to take an extra special trip, probably every other year, if they wanted to.

Their five-year plan ended in their second period. After five years, when Bill was 63, they could change their monthly withdrawals from Bill's IRA without any penalty and take out more or less or an extra lump sum at any time. They could also tap into any other of their resources as they needed to. They would set up another plan and budget their income needs and figure out from where to take their income at that time.

Their third time period starts at Bill's age $70\frac{1}{2}$, when they are required by law to take increasing minimum distributions from his IRA. This minimum starts at about 4.3% if both spouses are still living and is designed to make the IRA owner take distribution of the entire IRA in about 24 years. All of these distributions are taxable income, and this is how the IRS makes sure it collects taxes on the money you earned and saved, tax-deferred, for retirement.

Both Bill and Pat are entitled to Social Security benefits. They could start drawing them at age 62 and get 80% of their full benefit or wait till age 65 and get 100% of their full benefit or wait till age 70 and get 108% of their full benefit. Social Security benefits are tax-free for a single taxpayer with less than $25,000 annual income or for a married couple with less than $32,000. If your total income exceeds either of these, then your Social Security income becomes taxable. (See Table 18.3.)

Table 18.3   Tax Status of Social Security Income Received

Tax Due	Single Person Total Income	Married Couple Total Income
No tax	$0–25,000	$0–32,000
50% of benefit is taxable	$25,000–34,000	$32,000–44,000
85% of benefit is taxable	Over $34,000	Over $44,000

Another Social Security rule to be aware of in planning your retirement income is that if you draw Social Security benefits before age 65 and have an earned income in excess of $10,080, you have to "give back" $1 of Social Security income received for every $2 earned in excess of $10,080. Over age 65, there is no "give back" requirement, and you can earn as much as you want. Notice that this "give back" rule applies only to earned income, not investment income.

With these two sets of rules in mind, Bill and Pat decided not to draw their Social Security benefits until they each reached age 70. As they studied their financial picture, one other fact became clear to them: They would never run out of money! They also saw that they needed to plan their estate so that their riches could be passed on to others efficiently and not be wasted. They realized they could now make substantial gifts to their children, to charities, and to support other useful purposes. (See chapter 19.)

Bill and Pat's financial advisor knew all the tax rules about how to withdraw money from their IRAs and Social Security and guided them as they set up their retirement income. This is what their investments and income actually looked like during their retirement.

First Period: Age 58–63

During the first period, from Bill's age 58 to 63, their income would come from the following sources:

Investment Portfolio and Cash Yield   **Income**

Bill's IRA   ($1,275,000 total)

                    $500,000 U.S. government bond fund (6.1%) $30,500

                    $450,000 quality corporate bond fund (6.8%)   30,600

                    $325,000 growth and income fund (2.5% income)   +$8,100

                        (average growth of 9% = $29,250/year)   69,200

                    Withdrawal from principal

                        (from growth and income fund)   10,800

                                              $80,000

Net change: $29,250 growth less $10,800 withdrawal = $18,450 *gain* per year.

Because Bill's IRA showed a net gain each year, even after taking out $80,000 a year, they increased their income slightly to $7,000 per month, or $84,000 per year. Therefore, they took $14,800 a year from principal—the growth and income fund— so the net gain was actually $14,450 per year ($29,250 - $14,800 = $14,450). Because the whole IRA was at one fund company, their advisor gave instructions to the company to pay out $2,500 a month from the U.S. government bond fund ($30,000 per year), $2,500 a month from the corporate bond fund ($30,000 per year), and $2,000 a month from the growth and income fund ($24,000 per year), as shown in table 18.4.

Table 18.4   Earnings and Withdrawals from Bill and Pat's Retirement Investments

Investment	Principal	Actual Earnings	Withdrawal Annual	Monthly
U.S. government	$500,000	$30,500	$30,000	$2,500
Corporate	450,000	30,500	30,000	2,500
Growth and income from cash reserves	325,000	29,250	24,000	2,000
	$1,275,000	$90,250	$84,000	$7,000

This portfolio arrangement met the rule to pay out substantially equal payments for five years. It also did not deplete the IRA, partly because 25% of it was invested in a growth fund.

During this time, their variable annuity continued to grow, tax-deferred, and so did Pat's IRA. Their tax-free bond fund was always available to them without penalty and tax-free, and their small savings account was also available.

Second Period: Age 63–70½

During their second time period, from Bill's age 63 to 70½, they increased their withdrawals from Bill's IRA to $8,000 a month. This used up just the (average) growth percentage in the account. They also took out $200,000 for a vacation home and twice made gifts of $10,000 to each of their two children.

Third Period: Age 70½

During their third time period, they did some very thorough and detailed investment planning, tax planning, and estate planning. This process is called "financial planning." They realized they had some new and very serious problems, serious unless they devised some solutions now, while they were still healthy and active:

1. Their estate was growing every year. They were now taking out $8,000 a month and it was still growing.
2. If they did nothing and both lived another 20 years (a reasonable assumption), their heirs could end up paying well over half their accumulated riches to the IRS in income taxes and estate taxes.
3. They needed a long-term strategy to preserve their wealth and reduce their taxes.
4. They wanted to involve their two children and six grandchildren in their plans.
5. They needed help and advice from their attorney, accountant, and financial advisor.

The details of their planning are the stuff of another book, but any good financial advisor can help you through the process. In brief, this is what they did:

1. They set up a living trust to avoid probate and establish management of their assets during their lifetimes and after their demise. The trust had provisions covering management of their assets during sickness, incompetency, and terminal illness. It also contained instructions regarding donation of organs and burial or cremation. It established their principal beneficiaries and bequests.
2. They set up a life insurance trust to pay their estate taxes and replace the value of the charitable gifts they planned to make.

3. They made substantial gifts to various charities, which made them feel good, reduced their estate for tax purposes, and generated tax deductions to help offset their increasingly heavy income taxes.

4. They brought in their children and grandchildren—as they became old enough—to learn about, and ultimately to manage, their estate. Their estate became a family enterprise to be managed for the benefit of all.

5. They brought in experts, got good advice, and built a useful and beautiful financial enterprise.

They were thoroughly enjoying their lives and they had become *rich by choice*.

Chapter 19
What Your Heirs Need to Know: Step 7

Did you get rich just so your heirs could spend all your money and have a good time? Now that you are rich, you have one final choice to make: whether or not to teach your heirs to know and appreciate the value of money, to know that it has no value of itself but, like a great apple tree that is planted (invested) and cared for wisely, it can shade and feed you and them all your lives.

You have the choice to teach your children and heirs that the wealth you have built will grow and continue to grow for generations. As you have learned in this book, if you have the right attitude, know where you are going, and have a map, you will get rich. But don't go alone. Take your family, your heirs, with you. You cannot be rich in a vacuum. Don't keep your plan a secret from your family. Tell them about your financial situation and teach them to handle your wealth responsibly, to steward it.

As you are accumulating money, you have to share with your family not just how to build wealth but also why. Communicate with them, teach them, get them interested. Let them see that you have a plan, a goal, and a purpose. Show them the long-term benefits of wealth, how to build it, use it, and maintain it. Eventually, they will be as interested as you are.

When the next generations get involved in your plan, you may want to, or need to, adjust your plan, change the goals somewhat, and re-examine the purpose. This is important so everyone feels included and has real enthusiasm for the project.

When everyone is included in your plan and you work out differences in ideas and find common ground and common goals, when you are all in agreement, your plan and your wealth can go on forever. That's a legacy to be proud of. That's being truly financially rich. That is success, and it brings with it a great sense of satisfaction and accomplishment for a job well done.

As your heirs, children and grandchildren, develop a responsible attitude toward this wealth and learn to manage it and then inherit it, they too will experience a great sense of satisfaction and achievement for a job well done. There is no greater feeling in life.

Chapter 20
Bringing It All Together

Success. Wealth. Abundance. The choices are there every day, starting with your first paycheck. This book has shown you how middle-income people just like yourself made the decision to look after their financial situation and build their wealth. We have illustrated effective investment strategies for people ages 22 to 54 and for income ranges from $40,000 to $120,000 per year.

Sandy was just 22 when she graduated from college and got her first job. Her financial plan was very simple. She decided to invest $2,000 into her IRA every year. She had no other plan or strategy. Her investment was tax-deductible every year and it was tax-deferred in her IRA, she invested in good long-term mutual funds for steady growth, and she can retire early if she chooses to.

Her mutual funds own stocks in U.S. corporations. Those companies' growth usually keeps up with, or exceeds, the rate of inflation. The IRA uses the tax laws, and her steady investing year after year takes advantage of the benefits of compound interest.

Bill and Pat never thought seriously about their financial future until they were expecting their first child. Bill was 30, and by making a series of intelligent financial moves, they started to build their wealth. They saw the need for it, made a simple plan, and followed it successfully, using all the steps in the financial planning process.

Charles and Cindy were 40 when they decided to take stock of their lives and see what their financial future looked like. They had a few small investments and two children ready for college. By re-arranging and consolidating their accounts and increasing their contributions to their retirement account, they developed a plan that would enable them to retire in comfort and also help their children meet their college expenses.

Dr. Dave was 45 when he started his financial plan. If everything goes well, he could retire at 60 or have an even larger estate and greater retirement income at 65. He has made good choices, and time is on his side.

Even 50-year-olds can take charge of their financial situation and build real wealth, as demonstrated by John and Cathy in chapter 10. These people's stories show that anyone can build real wealth, have a comfortable retirement, pay for college, and enjoy life based on a solid financial foundation. So can you.

So can you.

About the Author

Erlend Peterson sold his graphics business and retired with his family to a 3.5-acre estate in Pasadena, California, complete with a swimming pool and tennis court. Four years later, he had spent all his money and had to go back to work.

He decided he needed to learn how to manage money, so he went into the personal money management and investment business, financial planning, in 1973. He became a certified financial planner in 1983 and now has clients all over the United States, Canada, and the Far East. He is also a registered investment advisor and manages millions of dollars in client portfolios.

He has 28 years' experience in investing and writing financial analyses and has given hundreds of seminars, most at major corporations. He has also served on the boards of the Institute of Certified Financial Planners and the International Association for Financial Practitioners, which have merged and formed the Financial Planning Association, the FPA.

He advises people on how to invest their money, when to buy insurance and how much they need, how to reduce their taxes, how to plan their retirement, and how to get the whole family involved so that when they pass on, their wealth is not wasted. *Rich by Choice* gives this same kind of financial advice to readers, almost as if they were sitting in his office.

Erlend Peterson and his partner, Michael Laine, can be reached at their offices in Culver City, California, phone (310) 568-4516. Their e-mail address is epeterson@afgweb.com. Both are Certified Financial Planners, and they provide financial and investment services and advice to clients across the United States and in many other countries.